AF589609

Published by UTU Media® - © 2026 Bridget Irby

ISBN - 9781966130000

Printed in the United States of America

Dear Reader,
This Book Is Dedicated To You.

Your journey may not always be easy but, it is worth it.
I hope you find the words inside helpful and healing.

When you need a break, color in a few of the built in coloring pages to calm your mind.

And remember, God and I both love you very much.

Dear Friend,

Have you ever felt it? That gentle whisper in your heart telling you that God has so much more for your life? That there's a deeper relationship with Him waiting just around the corner, if only you knew how to get there?

Maybe you're doing all the "right" things. You're reading your Bible (or at least trying to), showing up to church (most Sundays), and praying (even if sometimes it feels like your prayers are hitting the ceiling and bouncing right back). Yet somehow, it feels like you're stuck in spiritual quicksand – the more you struggle, the deeper you sink.

Here's the truth: Sometimes, the path to more of God isn't about doing more things right – ***it's about stopping the things that are holding you back***.

This is exactly why I created the "You Are Not Called" series. These books aren't about adding more to your spiritual to-do list. Instead, they're about gaining freedom by doing less – freedom from anxiety that steals your peace, freedom from fear that holds you captive, freedom from anger that robs your joy, freedom from shame that keeps you hidden, and freedom from loneliness that makes you feel disconnected from God and others.

I'm not writing these books from some lofty spiritual mountaintop. I'm writing as someone who has crawled through the valleys of anxiety, fear, anger, shame, and loneliness – and discovered that God was there all along, waiting to show me a better way. As an ordained minister, yes, but more importantly, as a woman who has lived every word on these pages, I can tell you with absolute certainty: You are not called to live this way. You are not called to be anxious, afraid, angry, ashamed, or alone. These struggles are not your inheritance as a child of God.

Think of this series as your spiritual "stop it" list. Just like a gardener needs to pull out weeds before planting new seeds, we need to identify and remove the things that are choking our spiritual growth.

I've seen God's transformative power firsthand. Each book in this series represents a battle I've fought and won, not through my own strength, but through discovering what God says about who we are and what we're called to be.

This journey won't always be easy but I promise you this: if you're ready to let go of what's holding you back, if you're willing to challenge the lies you've believed, and if you're prepared to step into the freedom God has for you, your life will never be the same. Because the truth is, sister, you were created for more than just surviving – you were created to thrive.

With faith, hope, and a whole lot of grace,

Bridget

XOXO

Christian Friends Are The Best Friends!

Hey Friend,

Before we dive into this journey of overcoming anger, I want to extend a special invitation to you. An invitation to not just read this book, but to truly live out its principles alongside other powerful Christian women.

You and I both know, we weren't meant to walk this path alone.

As Ecclesiastes 4:12 reminds us, "Though one may be overpowered, two can defend themselves. A cord of three strands is not quickly broken." This wisdom isn't just for ancient times - it's for us, right here, right now.

That's why I want to invite you to do life with me and other women just like you inside The Sisterhood. If you don't already have a strong support group of sound-minded, Christ-led sisters who inspire, uplift, and challenge you to live out your highest life, this is for you.

The Sisterhood is more than just a community - it's a place where we do life together. It's where we laugh, cry, pray, and grow side by side. It's where we put into practice the very principles you'll be reading about in this book.

Imagine having a group of sisters who:

- Pray, cry, and laugh with you through all of life's twists and turns
- Celebrate with you as you deepen your relationship with Christ
- Offer wise counsel to you when life gets complicated
- Stand with you in prayer as you pursue your God-given calling

This is what we do in The Sisterhood. Together, we're building the village that we all need. Just visit www.missiondrivensisters.com to join.

Remember, you weren't meant to do this alone. Let's link arms and become that unbreakable three-strand cord together!

Lots of love,

Bridget

XOXO

Hey there, superstar!

I'm so proud of you for starting this journey and because I'm not about to send you out there empty-handed, I've got some awesome resources to help you on your way to freedom from anger.

Think of these as your anger management toolkit. They're like the Swiss Army knife of emotional growth - versatile, handy, and they might just save you in a pinch (though maybe don't try to use them to open a can or cut down a small tree).

To access the resources, simply create your free account at www.youarenotcalled.com.

Inside, you'll have to the above resources plus much more!

Inside The Member's Area You'll Find:

- **Scripture Guide for Anger Management** It's packed with verses to help you find peace when you're about to lose your cool.

- **Daily Reflection Journal:** Ready to dig deeper into your anger triggers and responses? Our 30-day Daily Reflection Journal is here to guide you. It's like having a therapist in your pocket, minus the hefty bill.

- **Anger Management Action Plan Template** Time to put those strategies into action! Our Anger Management Action Plan Template will help you create a personalized roadmap to calmer days.

- **"Calm Down" Toolkit** Need a quick cool-down? Our 'Calm Down' Toolkit is your one-stop shop for de-escalating anger in the heat of the moment.

- **Relationship Repair Worksheet** Oops, did your anger cause some relationship hiccups? Our Relationship Repair Worksheet is here to help you smooth things over.

- **Generational Patterns Workbook** Ready to break free from your family's anger legacy? Our Generational Patterns Workbook will guide you through identifying and addressing those inherited anger habits.

- **Physical Relaxation Techniques Cheat Sheet** Want a quick reference guide for all those body-based calming techniques? Our Physical Relaxation Techniques Cheat Sheet has got you covered.

- **Prayer Guide for Overcoming Anger** Need some divine intervention in your anger management journey? Our Prayer Guide for Overcoming Anger is here to help you connect with God and find His peace.

Get access to everything above plus extras for free at www.YouAreNotCalled.com

A Not-So-Boring-But-Very-Important Disclaimer

(Please Read This, Even If You Usually Skip These Things)

Before we dive into this adventure together, we need to have a little chat. You know, the kind that usually comes with a cup of coffee and a "Now, don't freak out, but..." opener. So, grab your beverage of choice (I won't judge if it's not coffee), and let's get real for a moment.

First things first: I am not a doctor, therapist, counselor, or any other type of licensed mental health professional. I know, shocking right? Despite my incredible ability to dispense wisdom and wit (if I do say so myself), my qualifications are more in the realm of "life experience" and "passionate Jesus follower" than "Ph.D. in Psychology."

This book, as awesome as it is (and trust me, it's pretty awesome), is not meant to replace the invaluable work of trained professionals. Think of it more as a heart-to-heart with a friend who's been there, done that, and got the t-shirt (and maybe a few therapy sessions) to prove it.

If you're dealing with severe anger issues, depression, anxiety, or any other mental health concerns, **please, please, PLEASE seek help from a qualified professional.** They have tools in their toolbox that go way beyond what I can offer here. *(Plus, they probably have comfier couches for you to sit on while you talk.)*

This book is meant to be a companion on your journey, not your only guide. It's like having a workout buddy – super helpful and motivating, but not a substitute for a trained physical therapist if you've got a serious injury.

So, if at any point while reading this book you think, "Wow, I could really use some professional help with this," then congratulations! You've just had an incredibly mature and self-aware moment. Seriously, give yourself a pat on the back, then go find yourself a therapist. Your future self will thank you.

Remember, seeking help is not a sign of weakness. It's a sign that you're brave enough to admit you don't have all the answers (welcome to the club, by the way) and smart enough to ask for guidance. That's the kind of wisdom that would make Solomon proud!

Now, with all that said, I truly believe that this book has the potential to be a powerful tool in your spiritual and emotional growth journey. Just think of it as one piece of your "becoming-the-best-version-of-yourself" puzzle, not the whole picture.

So, are we clear? This book = awesome friend and spiritual cheerleader. Trained professionals = necessary allies for serious stuff. You = amazing child of God who deserves all the help and support you can get.

Alright, now that we've got that out of the way, let's get back to the good stuff. You've got a life-changing journey ahead of you, and I, for one, can't wait to see where it takes you. Just remember, if the road gets too bumpy, don't be afraid to call in some professional reinforcements. After all, even Batman needed Alfred, right?

Remember...

There's no rush.

You and me, love, we've got our whole lives to figure this thing out. Don't let rushing steal your joy.

There's no wrong answer.

This is unique to you and you simply cannot get it wrong. Just be honest with yourself and we can go from there.

You are doing great.

High five sister! Just the fact that you are here, with God, working on you says everything. Congratulations!

What's inside:

Introduction

I think everyone grows up in homes that are dysfunctional in some way or another. For me, I grew up thinking that yelling was normal. I believed that is just how people communicated.

Everyone in my life yelled. My parents yelled at each other. My grandparents yelled at each other. My grandparents yelled at my aunts and uncles. It's just how we existed.

As I got older and had my son, guess what I did?

I was a yeller. *Shocker...I know.* As a young single mom, I was extraordinarily overwhelmed by life. The bills, the cleaning, and all the requirements that came with having a small child and a demanding job were too heavy for me to carry.

Instead of figuring out how to manage my emotions so that my inner chaos didn't impact the people around me, I unleashed my anger on those closest to me from time to time. If you're anything like I was, sometimes you lose your cool. Sometimes, your emotions get the best of you. Sometimes, you say things that you wish you could take back.

If you're ready for that to change, I've got good news. You can absolutely achieve that goal. You can be in complete control of your emotions. You can make the shifts necessary to make the outbursts and overwhelm almost non-existent. And even better, it all starts right now.

The first thing you need to know is that it's not your fault. Feeling overwhelmed by life and triggered by things and unable to let things go is not an uncommon occurrence today. Why is that, you ask?

Because the devil is a liar, sister. He wants nothing more than to keep you stuck, hurting, and confused on how to overcome the things that are holding you back. Even more, he wants you to believe his lies and he is sneaky, sister. He weaves his lies with truths so they become so hard to detect.

Let me ask you something. Have you ever thought about what you're thinking about or what you believe to be true? Maybe you have, maybe you haven't. Either way, let's explore a few of the lies that you might have fallen into the trap of believing. Here's a few lies that I used to believe:

I can't stop getting angry. I have no control over it. It overwhelms me and is unstoppable.

I have a reason to be angry. You don't know what happened, what they did to me. Anyone would be angry. My anger is 100% justified.

Everyone yells or has outbursts sometimes. If they say they don't, they're just lying.

How am I supposed to not be angry when my husband doesn't do what I ask or my kids don't do what they're supposed to? If everyone did what they were supposed to and what is right, I wouldn't have a reason to yell. I wouldn't be angry then. They are the real problem.

This is just how I am. I am more emotional than other people. Love me or hate me, this is me.

Do you believe any of those lies? What other lies do you believe? Are there other stories that the enemy convinced you are truths?

Here's the important thing to always remember: The enemy wants to separate you from God. He wants to cause distance between you and the gifts that God has for you. Why? Because the more equipped you are by being in relationship and closeness with God, the more that you will advance God's kingdom.

So what do I mean by that? Remember how we talked about the fruit of the spirit in the introduction? The fruit of the spirit includes amazing things like love, joy, and peace. Have you ever seen an angry person who is also peaceful? No. Because if you have one, you can't have the other.

That's what the enemy wants. When we give in to our anger by believing that this is just how we are or that we are not at fault, we allow the enemy to separate us from the gifts we received through Christ.

Think of it this way. Giving over to anger is kind of like refusing to accept a gift from someone who loves you. Imagine a father who has sacrificed everything to give their child a shiny new truck for Christmas. He scrimped and saved and sacrificed to be able to buy his child a truck - the one that he'd always wanted. Yet, when the child receives the truck, he plays with it for a moment but quickly throws it in the back of the closet where it gets buried under all the other toys that he doesn't play with. Even though the child wants to play with the truck, because he doesn't see it, he thinks it's lost forever. Eventually, he forgets that the truck even exists. It's like he never had it at all.

That's the same thing the enemy does with our peace. When we first get saved and experience the Holy Spirit, it's easy to be peaceful. It's easy to love. It's easy to experience joy. Yet, as time goes on things change.

It's not as easy to be peaceful when the bills are more than the bank account. It's not easy to be joyful when all your off time is spent doing laundry, mopping floors, and scrubbing toilets. It's not easy to be loving and kind when you see that person who hurt you succeed. That's what the enemy counts on.

He counts on you to not have the knowledge on how to hold your peace and release your anger because that is what he wants. He wants you to eventually forget you have access to your shiny new truck in your closet.

He wants you to forget that you, as a child of God, have been given the gifts of God - peace, love, joy, patience, kindness, and more. He wants you to leave them in the closet, hidden under a mound of your past hurts, struggles, and pain.

He wants you to forget that they even belong to you. He wants you to look at all the other toys that are being played with and be sad that you don't have the same thing when in reality, you have everything you need.

But, you're too smart for his tricks. He may have fooled you for a minute but he won't fool you anymore.

You see, when Jesus died on the cross and paid our sacrifice, we became heirs to a certain heavenly inheritance. There is nothing you can do to earn it. There is nothing you can do to buy it. It is simply yours. There's no prerequisite study, no specific number of days you need to be saved to acquire these gifts. As a child of God, you are entitled to peace, love, and joy all the time.

It's kind of like an organ transplant. When Jesus paid the price for our sins and we enter into a covenant with God through his sacrifice, the cost has been paid. It's as if we needed an organ transplant desperately to live. We have a donor and the organ is there waiting for us. This organ will improve our quality of life.

It will allow us to run faster, leap higher, and breathe easier. Yet, we have the choice whether we will enter the hospital and receive our transplant or not. Yes, there will be some pain. Yes, our bodies will have to adjust to our new organ. We'll grow new vessels to strengthen and encourage our new growth. In the end, we'll come out the other side better, stronger, and more in alignment with who we were put on this earth to be.

So that's what we're going to do over the next few weeks. We're going to the hospital. We're getting our organ transplant. We're digging our truck out of the closet. We're accessing the gifts that Jesus died to give us. We're becoming tools for the kingdom and winning the war against the enemy. I can't promise you that it'll be easy but I can promise you that God and I will be there with you every step of the way.

So let's dive in...

Week One

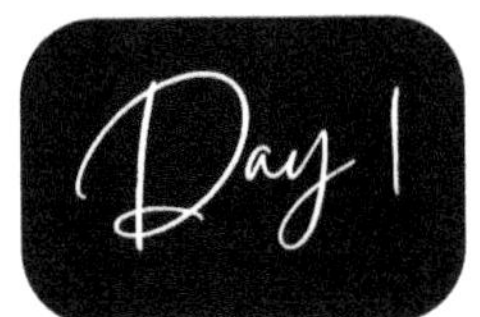

Be ye angry, and sin not: let not the sun go down upon your wrath: neither give place to the devil.
- EPHESIANS 4:26-27 (KJV)

If you'd asked me fifteen years ago, "Bridget, what do you think you'll be doing in the future?" I can guarantee that "writing a book to help women who love Jesus find peace, release, love, and joy" would not have been on my bingo card. Seriously, it would have been about as likely as me becoming a professional yodeler or mastering the art of underwater basket weaving.

Why? Because the devil had a million footholds in my life, anger being one of them.

At that time, I was a single mom, treading water in the deep end of life's pool, desperately trying not to drown. The concept of "future" felt about as relevant to me as a ski jacket in the Sahara. I was too busy surviving minute by minute to even consider what the next hour might bring, let alone the next year or decade.

And here's a little secret for you – a confession, if you will. During that season of my life, I truly believed that God didn't love me. The God I'd heard about in church, the one who was supposed to be all-loving and all-powerful, seemed completely disconnected from the God I was experiencing in my daily life.

I was angry. No, scratch that – I was furious. I felt like I had done everything I was "supposed" to do. I was kind to others (most of the time), had a genuinely good heart (I think), and wanted to help people (when I wasn't fantasizing about them mysteriously disappearing). I wanted to do God's will (or at least what I thought was God's will – spoiler alert: it's not always what we think it is).

Yet, no matter how hard I tried, my life was a daily struggle. Some days, I didn't even have the will to fight. It was like being stuck in a cosmic game of "Whack-a-Mole," where I was definitely the mole, and life was wielding a particularly enthusiastic mallet.

The weight of it all – the bills piling up faster than I could say "ramen noodles for dinner again," my partner's struggles with addiction, my son's behavior problems that made me wonder if he was secretly training to be a tiny dictator, the stress at work that made me contemplate faking my own disappearance and starting a new life as a hermit in the Himalayas, and my bank account which was emptier than my will to keep going – it all felt like too much to bear.

But here's the thing: God wasn't done with me yet. He had plans, big plans, that I couldn't even begin to imagine. And *he's not done with you yet either*. Trust me on this, His plans are way better than anything you could come up with on your own.

Can you relate to feeling overwhelmed by life circumstances? How has this affected your anger levels?

Have you ever felt like God didn't love you or that He was punishing you for something? How did that affect your emotions, particularly your anger?

What are your current strategies for dealing with anger? Are they working?

How might truly believing in God's unconditional love change how you handle anger?

Bible Reading

READ ACTS 9:1-19 (KJV)

Saul, later known as Paul, had a dramatic encounter with Jesus that completely changed his life. Before this encounter, Saul was filled with anger and hatred towards Christians. He actively persecuted them, believing he was doing God's will. But God had other plans.

How would you describe Saul's attitude and actions before his encounter with Jesus?

Do you think Saul would have ever thought that God would use him in such a tremendous way?

In what areas of your life might God be calling you to recognize a need for change?

Challenge

Start an "Anger Journal." When you feel angry, jot down what triggered it and how intense the feeling was. This awareness is the first step toward change.

Remember...

God's love for you is bigger than your biggest mistake, and His grace is more powerful than your strongest emotion. Even if that emotion is currently telling you to flip a table. (Pro tip: Don't flip the table. It never ends well.)

For I am persuaded, that neither death, nor life, nor angels, nor principalities, nor powers, nor things present, nor things to come, nor height, nor depth, nor any other creature, shall be able to separate us from the love of God, which is in Christ Jesus our Lord.
- Romans 8:38-39 (KJV)

I can vividly remember one night, sitting on my bathroom floor after a particularly challenging bedtime routine with my two-year-old. (Side note: whoever coined the term "terrible twos" was clearly an optimist.) I was surrounded by a sea of tears – mine, not my toddler's, for once.

At that moment, I did something I hadn't done in a while. I cried out to God. And let me tell you, it wasn't a pretty, poetic prayer. It was raw, it was messy, and it probably wouldn't have made it into a Christian inspirational quote calendar.

"I can't do this anymore, God," I sobbed. "I won't do this anymore. I thought you were a good God... but obviously I was wrong. I thought you loved me, but look at this nightmare that I live every day. No one would do this to someone they love..."

As soon as I'd finished my outburst (which, let's be honest, was more of a spiritual temper tantrum), something strange happened. My sobs subsided. My tears stopped flowing. It was as if someone had hit the mute button on my despair.

And then, in the silence of my heart, I heard Him. Not in a booming, Morgan Freeman-esque voice (although that would have been cool), but in a gentle whisper that somehow managed to drown out all my doubts and fears. He said: ***"My child, this is not the life I have for you. This is the life you chose when you turned from me."***

Whoa. Talk about a mic drop moment. Take a breath. No, seriously. Take a deep breath. Now read that again: *"My child, this is not the life I have for you. This is the life you chose when you turned from me."*

Mind. Blown. It was like God had just held up a mirror, and for the first time in forever, I could see clearly. How many times a day had I made choices that took me further away from the plans God had for my life? How often had I stubbornly insisted on doing things my way, only to end up lost and frustrated?

That moment marked the beginning of a journey I'm still on right now. I'm still learning how to keep my eyes fixed on Jesus, how to access the blessings He has for me, and how to co-create the life He longs for me to have. And let me tell you, it's been quite the adventure – like trying to assemble IKEA furniture without instructions, but infinitely more rewarding.

Have you ever had a "bathroom floor moment" with God? If so, what did you learn?

Is there anywhere in your life that you're making decisions and doing things your way but not satisfied with the results?

What are some areas of your life you'd like to give God control over?

How does the idea that God is close to the brokenhearted change your perspective on difficult times?

Bible Reading

READ JONAH 1:1-3 (KJV)

Jonah was a reluctant prophet of God who was called to deliver a message of repentance to the city of Nineveh. But, you see, Nineveh was the capital of Assyria, Israel's greatest enemy at the time. Because Jonah disliked the people of Nineveh so much, he was reluctant to follow God's command.

What did Jonah do when the Lord told him to go to Nineveh?

Are there any areas in your life that God has given you commands but your response is similar to Jonah's?

How might your life look different if you consistently chose God's path over your own?

Today's Challenge

Write a letter to God expressing your honest questions about your life, your circumstances, your past hurts, and anything that you don't understand or are angry about. Don't hold back – He can handle your raw emotions.

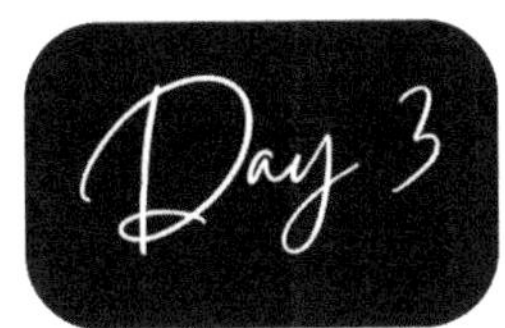

Take us the foxes, The little foxes, That spoil the vines: For our vines have tender grapes.

- Song of Solomon 2:15 (KJV)

I realized something when I was laying on the bathroom floor that night. I realized in a million different ways I was choosing the life that I had. I had chosen to separate myself from God's will without even realizing it. While I thought I was living for God and trying to do my best, the reality is that fear had kept me in a relationship that I knew wasn't of God.

Doubt in God's ability had kept me playing small in my career. Pride had kept me struggling behind quiet smiles and short answers when really, being a mom was the hardest thing I'd ever faced. Removing from your life the things (like anger) that separate you from God will cause a radical shift in ways you couldn't possibly imagine. Now, you might be thinking, "Oh, she's talking about the big, scary sins." But here's the twist – it's the "small" things that create the biggest distance. Things like a little anger, a touch of pride, a dollop of doubt, a bit of frustration, a dash of gossip, a sprinkle of shame. We might think they're not really that big of a deal, but trust me, they add up faster than calories on a Big Mac.

I don't say this to shame you, sis. Trust me, I've dealt with enough shame in my life to know it's a burden I wouldn't wish on anyone. I simply share this because if you want to access all that God has for you, you have to choose God's life over one of your own design. Choosing God's life begins with understanding what is not of God so you can access what is of God.

So, lean in with me here for just a moment. Close your eyes (well, maybe finish reading this paragraph first – safety first!), and imagine a day where you wake up totally peaceful. You're not worried about what's to come. Your mind isn't filled with the endless to-do list of the day. You're not stressed about whether you sent that email, or clocked out, or what your family thought about that thing you said three weeks ago that you're still obsessing over. All your worries and concerns have been replaced with total peace.

As you get ready for the day, nothing phases you. The dirty dishes in the sink? No biggie. The pile of laundry waiting to be folded? It can wait. The kids screaming like they're auditioning for a heavy metal band? Just background music. The Lego you just stepped on? Okay, that still hurts, but you don't even consider yelling. The unreturned text message from a friend? You'll get to it when you can. You, my love, are unphased and at peace. You are non-triggerable. You go throughout your day as your highest and best self, completely in control of your emotions and never losing your peace.

Sounds like a fantasy, right? Like something out of a cheesy self-help book or a particularly optimistic fortune cookie? Well, hold onto your hats, because that is exactly what God has for you.

What are some "small things" in your life that might be creating distance between you and God?

How have these seemingly minor issues affected your relationship with God over time?

What's the biggest obstacle between you and the peaceful day described above?

What's one small change you could make to invite more peace into your daily routine?

Bible Reading

READ COLOSSIANS 3:1-17 (KJV)

Putting away sinful behaviors and thoughts acts as both a blessing and a protective bubble around our lives and brings us closer to God. By living a transformed life, our lives serve as a powerful testimony to the reality and power of Christ.

How does Paul's instruction to "set your minds on things above" relate to putting to death the old sinful nature? Can you give a practical example of how you might do this in your daily life?

Paul lists several virtues to "put on" as part of the new self. Which of these do you find most challenging, and what steps could you take to cultivate this virtue?

How might your relationships and daily interactions change if you consistently applied the principles in this passage, particularly the instruction to "let the peace of Christ rule in your hearts" and to forgive as the Lord forgave you?

Challenge

Do a "spiritual clutter clean-up." Just like you'd declutter a closet, take some time to identify and "remove" small spiritual clutter in your life. This could be negative self-talk, a gossiping habit, or holding onto small grudges.

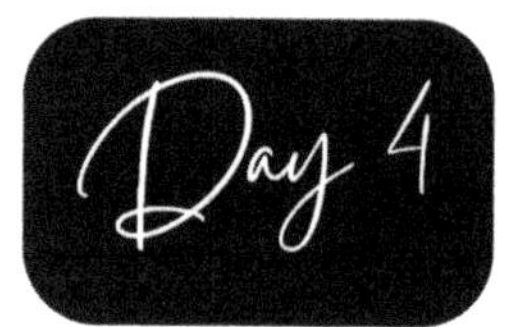

But the fruit of the Spirit is love, joy, peace, longsuffering, gentleness, goodness, faith, meekness, temperance: against such there is no law.
- Galatians 5:22-23 (KJV)

In Galatians 5:22, the Bible tells us what kind of fruit the Holy Spirit produces in our lives. The fruit of the Spirit consists of love, joy, peace, patience, kindness, goodness, faithfulness, gentleness, and self-control. It's like the ultimate personality makeover, courtesy of the Holy Spirit.

Can you imagine going through life with all of those all the time? It's like having a superpower, but instead of flying or turning invisible, you have the ability to not lose your cool when the barista gets your coffee order wrong for the third time this week.

Even more, it's your right as a child of God to have these things. In John 10:10, Jesus says, "I came that they may have life, and have it abundantly." That means you, friend. You are the worthy investment that Jesus chose so long ago. If he believed you were worth it and that it was possible for you then you should too.

Let's break these fruits down. Imagine if your life was a smoothie, and these were the ingredients:

- **Love**: Not the Hollywood rom-com kind, but the "I'll help you move on a Saturday" kind.
- **Joy**: This isn't just being happy when things go your way. It's more like having an unshakeable good mood, even when your coffee maker breaks and you stub your toe... on the same morning.
- **Peace**: Picture the calmest person you know. Now picture them in the middle of a Black Friday sale. That level of chill? That's what we're aiming for.
- **Patience** (aka Forbearance): It's what you need when you're explaining technology to your grandparents or waiting for your teenager to clean their room. Superhuman levels of not losing your cool.
- **Kindness**: This is like niceness, but with bonus points. It's going out of your way to make someone's day better, even if that someone is the person who always steals your parking spot.
- **Goodness**: Not just doing the right thing, but doing it with pizzazz. It's like moral excellence with jazz hands.
- **Faithfulness**: This is trusting and loving God through all your circumstances because you stick to God like your life depends on it. Because, spiritually speaking, it kind of does.
- **Gentleness**: Imagine if a cloud and a kitten had a baby. That's the level of softness we're talking about here.
- **Self-control**: This is your inner adult, the one that says, "Maybe we don't need that fourth slice of cake" or "Let's not send that angry email just yet." I know...she gets on my nerves, too.

Can you imagine not being overcome with anger when you're feeling overwhelmed or attacked? Picture yourself staying calm and collected when your toddler decides to use your freshly painted walls as their personal art canvas.

Can you imagine not being paralyzed by fear when you want to ask for that raise or promotion, or when you need to tell your friend that their constant negativity is bringing you down? Imagine approaching your boss with the confidence of a toddler in a Superman costume.

Can you imagine not feeling shame regarding your past mistakes? Think about walking into a room without the weight of your past failures trying to convince you that you don't belong there.

Can you imagine feeling like you are worthy of the love of the living God? Because spoiler alert: you absolutely are.

Whether you can imagine it right now or not, I can promise you that living with the fruit of the Holy Spirit is possible for you. *Will it always be easy?* About as easy as trying to herd cats in the rain.

But here's the good news: we serve a loving, patient, and kind God who is more than willing to take our hand and lead the way to the life He wants us to live.

Reflection

Which fruit of the Spirit do you find most challenging to exhibit when you're angry?

Which fruit of the Spirit do you most need to cultivate in your life right now? Why?

How might emphasizing these fruits change your response to anger triggers?

Bible Reading

READ GALATIANS 5:16-25 (KJV)

Paul contrasts the works of the flesh with the fruit of the Spirit. He urges believers to live by the Spirit, which means allowing the Holy Spirit to guide their actions and attitudes. Paul lists specific behaviors to avoid and then describes the positive characteristics (love, joy, peace, etc.) that will be evident in a Spirit-led life.

Paul talks about a conflict between the flesh and the Spirit. How have you experienced this struggle in your own life, and what strategies have you found helpful in "walking by the Spirit"?

Paul states that "those who belong to Christ Jesus have crucified the flesh with its passions and desires" (v.24). What do you think this means practically, and how does it relate to the ongoing process of living by the Spirit?

Today's Challenge

Create a visual reminder of the fruits of the Spirit. This could be a drawing, a list on your mirror, or even a literal fruit bowl with each fruit labeled. Place it somewhere you'll see it often.

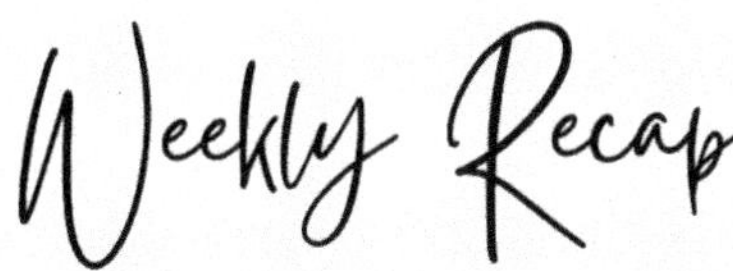

Over these past four days, we've embarked on a transformative journey from anger to peace. Let's revisit the key points we've covered:

- Change: We acknowledged that anger often stems from feeling overwhelmed and disconnected from God's love. We learned that God sees us, even in our messiest moments, and has a better plan for our lives.
- Love: We explored the powerful truth that God loves us, even when we're angry. We discovered that our "bathroom floor moments" can be turning points in our relationship with God.
- Distance: We identified how seemingly minor issues like frustration, gossip, and shame can create significant barriers between us and God. We envisioned what a day filled with God's peace might look like.
- Fruit: We delved into the nine fruits of the Spirit and how cultivating these can transform our responses to anger-inducing situations.

Deeper Dive

You've taken the first steps on this journey from anger to peace. But remember, this is just the beginning. Here are some suggestions for continuing your growth:

- Keep Your Anger Journal: Continue to track your anger triggers and your responses. Over time, you'll see patterns emerge. You can access your free 30 day anger journal and other resources at youarenotcalled.com.
- Daily Fruit Check: Each day, focus on exhibiting one fruit of the Spirit. Journal about your experiences and challenges.
- Scripture Memorization: Commit key verses we've studied to memory. Start with Ephesians 4:26-27 and Galatians 5:22-23.
- Accountability Partner: Find a trusted friend or family member to share this journey with. Regular check-ins can help you stay on track and provide encouragement.
- Pray Continuously: Make it a habit to turn to God in all moments, not just the difficult ones. Cultivate an ongoing conversation with Him throughout your day.

Week Two

Now the Lord is that Spirit: and where the Spirit of the Lord is, there is liberty.
- 2 Corinthians 3:17 (KJV)

Picture this: Sarah, a young woman with a penchant for poor life choices (hey, we've all been there), finds herself in a bit of a pickle. And by "pickle," I mean she's committed a crime that comes with a side of "go directly to jail, do not pass Go, do not collect $200." Yikes.

But wait! Enter Elena, Sarah's mom, stage left. Now, Elena's not your average mom. She's more like a superhero in mom jeans.

When the truth about Sarah's crime comes out, Elena pulls a move straight out of a feel-good movie. She steps forward and says, "It was me. I did it."

I know what you're thinking. "Elena, girl, what are you doing?" But Elena's got a plan. She figures Sarah's got her whole life ahead of her, and she'd rather sacrifice her freedom than see her daughter waste away behind bars. Talk about a mother's love, right?

So, fast forward a bit. Elena's rocking an orange jumpsuit, and Sarah? Well, Sarah's free as a bird. But here's where our story takes a turn from touching to tragically comedic.

Sarah, bless her heart, can't seem to get with the program. Instead of embracing her newfound freedom and living her best life, she's camped outside the prison like it's Black Friday and she's waiting for a doorbuster deal. Day after day, she's there, staring at those grim prison walls like they hold the secrets to the universe.

Passersby start to notice. They're probably thinking, "Is this some new form of performance art? Is she protesting something? Or maybe she just really likes concrete?" Little do they know, they're witnessing a living, breathing metaphor for how many of us treat the freedom Christ gave us.

How many of us are pulling a Sarah when it comes to anger? We've been given this incredible gift of freedom in Christ, but instead of running with it, we're standing outside the prison of our past hurts, resentments, and anger, unable to move forward.

It's like we've won an all-expenses-paid vacation to Hawaii, but we're too busy reorganizing our sock drawer to go.

In what ways can you relate to Sarah in this story? Are there areas in your life where you're not fully embracing your freedom in Christ?

How does Elena's sacrifice for Sarah mirror what Christ did for us? How does this perspective impact your view of your own freedom?

What "prison walls" might you be staring at in your own life? What's keeping you from walking away from them?

Bible Reading

READ LUKE 15:11-32 (KJV)

This parable shares some similarities with our story of Sarah and Elena. The prodigal son, like Sarah, makes poor choices. The father, like Elena (and ultimately, like God), offers undeserved grace and freedom.

How does the prodigal son's reaction to his father's forgiveness differ from Sarah's reaction to her freedom?

What can we learn from the father's response to his son's return?

How might the older brother's anger relate to our own struggles with fully embracing God's grace and freedom?

Challenge

Identify one "prison wall" of anger in your life - a past hurt, a grudge, a persistent frustration - that you've been staring at instead of walking away from. Write it down, pray over it, and make a conscious decision to take one step away from it today.

Remember...

Remember, embracing your freedom from anger is a daily choice. It might feel uncomfortable at first, like Sarah leaving her spot outside the prison. But with each step, you're moving towards the life of freedom God intends for you.

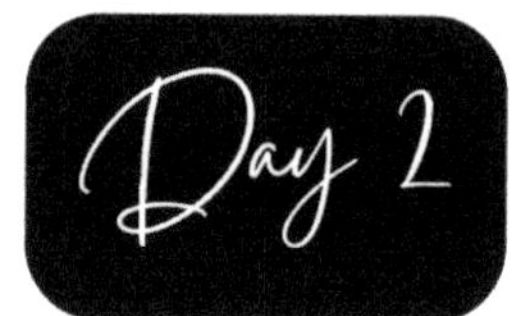

Be ye angry, and sin not: let not the sun go down upon your wrath: neither give place to the devil.
- Ephesians 4:26-27 (KJV)

Alright, let's play a game of "Spot the Anger." It's like Where's Waldo, but instead of a guy in a striped shirt, we're looking for sneaky forms of anger that often go undetected. Ready? Let's go!

Anger isn't always the red-faced, steam-coming-out-of-your-ears kind of thing. Sometimes it's sneakier:

- Bitterness: This is like anger that's been left out in the sun too long. It's sour, it's unpleasant, and nobody wants to be around it.
- Resentment: This is when you're still mad about something that happened three years ago. It's like anger with frequent flyer miles.
- Frustration: This is anger's annoying little brother. It's what happens when you try to assemble IKEA furniture without instructions.
- Hate: This is anger that's been working out at the gym. It's buff, it's intense, and it's not afraid to show off.
- Silence: Sometimes anger goes incognito. It's the cold shoulder, the silent treatment, the "I'm fine" when you're clearly not fine.
- Indifference: This is anger in disguise. It's pretending not to care when you actually care a whole lot.

Let's look at a few examples: Meet Sarah (not the same Sarah from our earlier story - apparently, it's a popular name). Sarah's a working mom who's constantly frustrated with her husband for not helping enough around the house. Her anger shows up as sarcasm sharper than a chef's knife and silent treatments colder than the Arctic.

Then there's Mark, a college student who's harboring more resentment towards his parents than a teenager who's had their phone confiscated. They pressured him into a major he hates, and now his anger is showing up as indifference towards his studies and a sudden inability to remember how to call home.

And let's not forget Lisa, a church volunteer who's bitter about always being the one stuck with clean-up duty. Her anger is manifesting as complaints to other volunteers and a sudden "allergy" to all future church events.

Which of these "faces" of anger do you most often wear? How has this affected your relationships?

Can you think of a time when you mistook one of these sneaky forms of anger for something else? What happened?

How might recognizing these different expressions of anger help you in managing your emotions better?

Bible Reading

READ GENESIS 4:1-16 (KJV)

Cain's anger towards his brother led to the first murder in the Bible. This story shows us the dangerous progression of unchecked anger.

What was the root cause of Cain's anger? How might he have handled his emotions differently?

How did God respond to Cain's anger before it led to action? What does this teach us about God's desire to help us manage our anger?

What were the consequences of Cain giving in to his anger? How does this relate to consequences we might face when we let anger control our actions?

Today's Challenge

Today, play detective with your emotions. When you feel upset, try to identify which "face" of anger you're experiencing. Create an "Anger Log." Every time you feel angry or one of its sneaky cousins (bitterness, resentment, etc.), write down what triggered the feeling and how you responded.

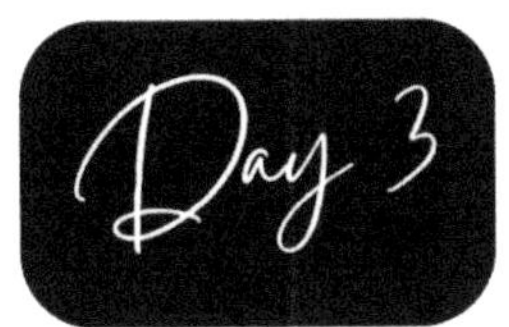

Wherefore, my beloved brethren, let every man be swift to hear, slow to speak, slow to wrath: for the wrath of man worketh not the righteousness of God.
- James 1:19-20 (KJV)

Now, let's talk about why anger pops up in the first place. Often, it's because there's a gap between what we expect and what actually happens. It's like ordering a gourmet burger and getting a soggy fish stick instead. Disappointment + Frustration = Anger. It's basic emotional math.

Anger can also come from a lack of forgiveness. Holding onto past hurts is like carrying around a bag of rotten vegetables. It stinks, it weighs you down, and eventually, it's going to make a mess.

So, who does anger really hurt? *Spoiler alert: it hurts everyone.*

- It hurts us: Anger is like drinking poison and expecting the other person to get sick. It robs us of peace, joy, and the ability to enjoy a good night's sleep without replaying arguments in our head.

- It hurts those around us: Angry people are about as fun to be around as a wet cat. Our anger can damage relationships, create tension, and make people avoid us like we have a contagious disease.

- It hurts our health: Chronic anger is like putting your body on a steady diet of stress and tension. It's a fast track to high blood pressure, headaches, and a general feeling of "Why do I feel like I've been hit by a truck?"

- It hurts our spiritual life: Anger can create a barrier between us and God thicker than the walls of Jericho. It's hard to hear God's still, small voice when our internal angry voice is shouting like a sports fan at a championship game.

- It hurts our witness: As Christians, we're supposed to be reflecting Christ. But when we're controlled by anger, we're reflecting something decidedly less divine. It's like trying to be a lighthouse while throwing rocks at passing ships.

Can you identify a recent situation where unmet expectations led to anger? How might you have handled it differently?

In what ways has holding onto anger affected your life? Your relationships? Your health?

How might letting go of anger improve your witness as a Christian?

Bible Reading

READ JONAH 4:1-11 (KJV)

Last week, we looked at what happened when God told Jonah to go to Nineveh. Now, we're looking at Jonah's response to the outcome at Nineveh. Jonah becomes angry when God shows mercy to the people of Nineveh, who he believed deserved punishment.

What were Jonah's expectations? How did they differ from God's plan?

How did Jonah's anger affect his relationship with God?

Is there any area in your life that you're angry about God's response? Maybe you expected things to go one way but they've gone another?

Challenge

Today, practice the P.A.U.S.E. method when you feel anger rising:
P - Pause and take a deep breath **A** - Acknowledge your feelings without judgment **U** - Understand your expectations and how they might be unrealistic **S** - Select a positive response **E** - Engage with the situation in a constructive way

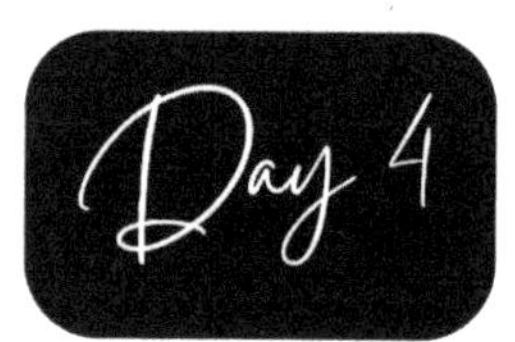

Wherefore, my beloved brethren, let every man be swift to hear, slow to speak, slow to wrath: for the wrath of man worketh not the righteousness of God.
- Ephesians 4:31-32 (KJV)

Imagine a potter working on a beautiful vase. She's almost done, it's looking gorgeous, and then... anger causes her hand to slip. Suddenly, that vase looks less like a masterpiece and more like modern art gone wrong. That's what anger does to the beautiful life God is crafting for us.

But here's the good news: we have an antidote to anger. It's not a magic pill or a secret potion. It's something much more powerful - forgiveness.

Now, I know what you're thinking. "Forgiveness? That's your big solution? I was hoping for something more along the lines of a Jedi mind trick or a time machine." I get it.

Forgiveness can seem like a weak response to the strong emotion of anger. But here's the thing - forgiveness is like a superhero in disguise. It might look mild-mannered on the outside, but it's packing some serious power.

Forgiveness doesn't mean what they did was okay. It doesn't mean you have to be best buddies with them or even have them in your life at all. Forgiveness is about releasing the hold that person and that hurt have on you. It's about choosing to lay down the heavy backpack of anger and resentment you've been lugging around.

Think about it this way: when you're angry at someone, who's really suffering? Sure, they might feel bad for a while, but chances are they're not losing sleep over it. Meanwhile, you're over here stewing in your own juices, replaying the incident over and over, letting it steal your peace and joy. Forgiveness is like pressing the 'delete' button on that mental recording. It's choosing freedom for yourself.

Forgiveness isn't always a warm, fuzzy feeling that magically appears – sometimes it's a down-and-dirty choice we have to make, even when everything in us is screaming to hold onto that grudge. You might be thinking, *"But Bridget, you don't understand. I want to punch them in the face, not forgive them!"* Trust me, I get it.

But remember: forgiveness isn't about them, it's about freeing yourself from the prison of anger and resentment and submitting your will to the will of God. So take a deep breath, grit your teeth if you have to, and choose forgiveness – your future self will thank you for it.

Reflection

What's the most difficult thing you've ever had to forgive?

How has holding onto unforgiveness affected your life and relationships?

In what ways might choosing forgiveness change your daily experience of anger?

Bible Reading

READ GENESIS 50:15-21 (KJV)

Joseph had every reason to be angry with his brothers who sold him into slavery. Yet, he chose forgiveness and saw God's bigger picture.

How did Joseph's perspective on his brothers' actions change over time?

What enabled Joseph to forgive such a significant betrayal?

How did Joseph's forgiveness impact his brothers and the larger story of God's people?

Today's Challenge

Today, create a "Freedom from Anger" action plan. Identify your top 3 anger triggers. For each trigger, write down: a fruit of the Spirit you can cultivate in response, a specific action you can take when faced with this trigger and a scripture you can meditate on related to this challenge

1. Log in to your member's area online so you can access this weeks group activity, discussion questions, and other resources to support your anger busting journey!

2. Get excited about next week because we'll dive deeper into practical strategies for managing anger in the heat of the moment. We'll explore techniques to cool down quickly, communicate effectively when emotions are high, and build habits that promote peace in our daily lives.

3. Remember, this journey of freedom from anger is ongoing. There will be setbacks, but don't let them discourage you. Each time you choose love over anger, patience over irritation, or forgiveness over resentment, you're taking a step toward the freedom and purpose God has for you.

Weekly Recap

- **Day 1: Understanding Anger and Its Impact**
  - We explored the story of Sarah and Elena, using it as a metaphor for how we often remain "imprisoned" by our anger even when freedom is available.
  - We learned that embracing freedom from anger is a daily choice, much like Sarah choosing to leave the prison walls behind.
- **Day 2: The Many Faces of Anger**
  - We discovered that anger isn't always obvious and can manifest as bitterness, resentment, frustration, hate, silence, or indifference.
  - We practiced being "anger detectives" to identify these sneaky forms of anger in our lives.
- **Day 3: The Domino Effect of Anger**
  - We examined how unmet expectations and lack of forgiveness often trigger anger.
  - We explored the wide-ranging impacts of anger on ourselves, our relationships, our health, our spiritual life, and our Christian witness.
  - We learned the P.A.U.S.E. method for managing anger in the moment.
- **Day 4: Overcoming Anger with Forgiveness**
  - We delved into forgiveness as a powerful antidote to anger.
  - We created personal "Freedom from Anger" action plans to begin practicing the art of forgiveness.

Week Three

He that is slow to anger is better than the mighty;
And he that ruleth his spirit than he that taketh a city.
- Proverbs 16:32 (KJV)

Have you ever found yourself in a situation where you're trying to do the right thing, but it feels like the universe is conspiring against you? Well, buckle up, because I'm about to take you on a wild ride through my own personal "blended family blender."

Picture this: my husband and I, two starry-eyed lovebirds, decide to combine our families. We each brought to the table a colorful history of previous partners, a grab bag of mistakes (buy one, get ten free!), and children to beautifully blend into one big happy family. It was going to be just like "The Brady Bunch," right?

Reality hit us faster than a toddler can destroy a freshly cleaned living room. Instead of harmonious family dinners and matching outfits, we found ourselves knee-deep in court battles over custody, child support, and everything in between. It was less "Brady Bunch" and more "Game of Thrones" – minus the dragons, thankfully.

I prayed to God constantly, asking Him to work things out. I imagined He'd wave His divine wand, and suddenly all our exes would become reasonable, cooperative individuals. Spoiler alert: that's not quite how it went down.

One day, I felt God pressing me to pray for our exes. Not just a quick "God bless 'em" as I rolled my eyes, but to get down on my knees and genuinely pray for each one. Every. Single. Day.

Now, let me tell you, this was not my idea of a good time. It felt about as appealing as voluntarily cleaning the bathroom with a toothbrush. But, being the obedient child of God that I occasionally remember to be, I decided to give it a shot.

📌 Reality Check:
When facing a challenging situation today, pause and ask yourself, "What's my 'Brady Bunch' expectation here, and what's the reality?" Recognizing the gap between our expectations and reality can help us respond more gracefully to disappointments.

Can you recall a time when your expectations for a situation were vastly different from the reality? How did you handle it?

In what areas of your life do you find yourself most prone to unrealistic expectations?

How might acknowledging the reality of a situation, rather than clinging to an idealized version, change your emotional response?

Have you ever been asked to do something for someone you were angry with? How did it feel initially, and did your feelings change over time?

Bible Reading

READ MATTHEW 5:43-45 (KJV)

God's not looking for our sacrifices or our perfectly curated Instagram-worthy Christian life. He wants our obedience, even when it's uncomfortable, messy, and makes us want to scream into a pillow. Trust me, though – choosing obedience over sacrifice might feel like swallowing a cactus at first, but it's always, always worth it in the end.

Choose 3-5 people who have recently frustrated or angered you. For each person, write down a specific blessing you can sincerely pray for them. It could be for their health, their family, their job, or their relationship with God. Spend a few minutes genuinely praying these blessings over each person.

Challenge

Identify an area in your life where you have high expectations. Write down your ideal outcome. Now, write down a possible scenario, considering potential challenges or limitations. Reflect on how you might respond gracefully if the realistic scenario occurs.

Remember...

Remember, managing our expectations doesn't mean we stop hoping for good things. It means we approach life with a flexibility that allows us to respond to reality with grace rather than anger. And choosing to pray for those who challenge us can profoundly impact our own hearts, even if it doesn't immediately change our circumstances.

But I say unto you which hear, Love your enemies, do good to them which hate you, bless them that curse you, and pray for them which despitefully use you.
- Luke 6:27-28 (KJV)

Picture me, on my knees, trying to pray sincerely for these people who seemed determined to make our lives as complicated as possible. I'm there, attempting to channel my inner saint, when my phone starts buzzing like an angry hornet. It's my partner's ex, sending text messages so venomous they could have powered a small city if we could harness the energy of spite.

In that moment, my prayers took on a slightly... creative tone. "*God, please bless her,*" I prayed through gritted teeth. "*Bless her all in her face. Bless her hard, Jesus, straight to the face. Just knock her over with blessings.*"

I'll admit, at first, I didn't exactly mean what I was saying. It was more like spiritual sarcasm. But you know what? God has a sense of humor too, and He's also pretty clever. As I kept up this prayer routine, something started to change. It wasn't the exes – oh no, they were still being their charming selves. It was me.

Slowly but surely, God began to soften my heart. Those sarcastic prayers started to become genuine. "Bless her all in her face" turned into "Help her find peace." "Knock her over with blessings" became "Show her Your love in a way she can't ignore."

This shift changed everything. The challenges that used to send me from zero to furious in 2.5 seconds started to lose their power. It was like God was going through my emotional control panel, removing buttons one by one. The "Instant Rage" button? Gone. The "Bitter Resentment" switch? Deactivated. The "Petty Revenge Fantasy" lever? Okay, He left that one, but pushed it way to the back where it's hard to reach.

Now, I'd love to tell you that after all this, our big blended family turned into a perfect harmony of love and understanding. But let's keep it real – it's still messy, still complicated. However, the change in me changed everything. I got my peace back. The anger and resentment that used to have me in a chokehold? They lost their grip.

Exploring the Emotional Control Panel Concept

Imagine your emotions as a complex control panel with various buttons, switches, and levers. Each one represents a different emotional response. Some might be labeled "Patience," "Kindness," or "Joy," while others might say "Anger," "Bitterness," or "Resentment."

The key is recognizing that you have the power to choose which controls to activate. Just because a situation pushes your buttons doesn't mean you have to push back. You can consciously decide which emotional response to engage.

What "buttons" on your emotional control panel tend to get pushed most often? Who or what usually pushes them?

Can you recall a time when you chose not to react to a trigger? How did it feel, and what was the outcome?

How might your relationships change if you could deactivate your buttons?

Bible Reading

READ PHILLIPPIANS 4:6-7 (KJV)

God's not telling us to stuff our feelings in a box and paste on a plastic smile. Nope, He's inviting us to bring the whole messy package to Him in prayer. Instead of letting our emotions drive us, God wants to take the driver's seat. When we hand over the keys to Him, that's when His peace guards our hearts and minds.

Can you recall a time when you let your emotions lead you instead of bringing them to God? What was the outcome, and how might it have been different if you had approached the situation with prayer?

The passage mentions "prayer and petition, with thanksgiving." How might incorporating gratitude into your prayers, even during stressful times, change your perspective and emotional state?

Keep In Mind...

Remember, changing our emotional responses is a process. It's okay if you don't get it right every time. The important thing is that you're becoming more aware of your choices and actively working to make better ones. You're rewiring your emotional responses, and that's a big deal!

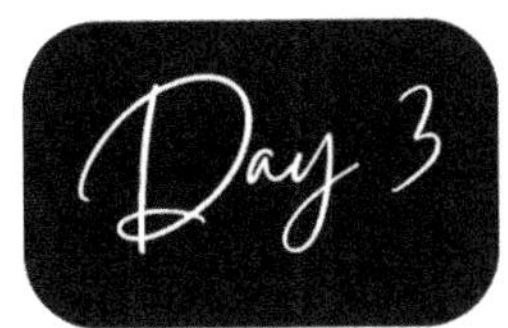

A soft answer turneth away wrath:
But grievous words stir up anger.
- Proverbs 15:1 (KJV)

Navigating life's challenges is kind of like driving a public bus. As you travel along your route through life, different passengers are constantly trying to board. There's Anger, Fear, Jealousy, and Doubt, just to name a few.

The thing that you have to remember as the driver is that every passenger you pick up has a different stop they want to get to. The longer they ride with you, the more urgent their need to arrive at their destination will be. And you have to ask yourself, is this passenger going somewhere that I actually want to go? Is this passenger's journey going to take me closer to or further from God's will for my life?

As the driver, you have the power and responsibility to choose who boards your bus. Even better, with God as your ever-present co-pilot, you can choose the passengers who will make your trip fun and fruitful.

Let's break it down with some everyday scenarios:

- **Anger**: Your coworker takes credit for your idea in a meeting. Anger runs up, red-faced and loud, promising a quick trip to Justification Junction. But remember, if you let him on, you will end up at Regret Ridge or Broken Relationship Bay. *Is that somewhere that you really want to be?*
- **Fear**: You're considering applying for a promotion. Fear tries to sneak on, whispering your insecurities in your ear. Her final stop? Missed Opportunity Mountain. *No growth and fruit there.*
- **Jealousy**: Your friend just bought a new car you've been eyeing. Jealousy looks flashy, tempting you with "what-ifs." But be careful - his route leads straight to Bitter Valley and Discontent Desert.
- **Doubt**: You're about to share your faith with a friend. Doubt shuffles on quietly, and before you know it, your silence has taken your friend's opportunity to know Jesus.

Now, here's the good news: Even if these passengers have snuck on board, you can kick them off at any time! Some emotions, like grief or chronic anxiety, might be long-term riders. While we can't always kick them off immediately, we can choose not to let them drive.

Remember: You are strong, resilient, and capable of more than you realize. If you need to reevaluate the passengers on your bus and make some adjustments, today is the day to start. It might feel challenging at first, but with practice and God's guidance, you'll become a master at navigating your route. And if you need help and support on your journey, professional resources and counseling aren't a bad idea.

Which "emotion passenger" frequently flags down your bus? What triggers their appearance?

Are there any emotional passengers on your bus that you need to kick off? If so, what is one step you can take today to start moving in that direction?

How might inviting God to be your co-pilot change your bus route?

Bible Reading

READ 1 SAMUEL 30:1-6 (KJV)

David faced a situation where Despair and Revenge were trying to board his bus. Instead, he chose to strengthen himself in the Lord, effectively kicking those passengers off and choosing a different direction.

What "emotional passengers" were trying to board David's bus?

How did David's choice to "strengthen himself in the Lord" redirect his journey?

How can we apply David's example to our own emotional bus routes?

Challenge

Today, create your own bus manual. Imagine your bus with God as co-pilot. List frequent emotional passengers and their intended destinations. For each, write a positive alternative destination. Throughout the day, think about your options when emotions try to board. At day's end, reflect on how this guided your choices. You'll find space on the next page to create your manual.

Emotional Passenger	Destination	Alternative Destination

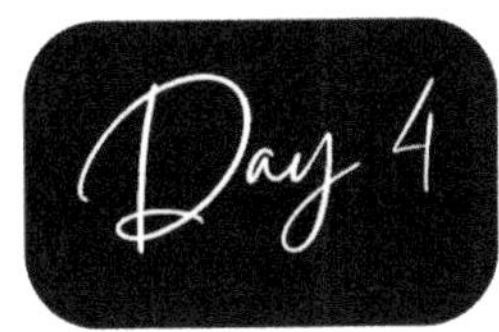

casting down imaginations, and every high thing that exalteth itself against the knowledge of God, and bringing into captivity every thought to the obedience of Christ.
2 Corinthians 10:5 (KJV)

Recognizing these passengers is the first step. The next step is remembering that you have the power to control who rides on your bus. You can watch these emotions roll in, acknowledge them – "Oh, look, here comes Anger again" – and then choose not to open the doors. If anger sneaks onto your bus anyway, you as the driver have the choice to just sit still and not go anywhere until Anger gets off your bus. Trust me, eventually Anger will give up and step off your bus in search for a more friendly situation that it can control.

But how do we do this in practice? Let's look at some practical spiritual and practical techniques that you can use every day to control your anger.

Spiritual Practices:

- *Prayer*: It doesn't have to be eloquent – even "God, help me not to lose it right now" counts!
- *Scripture*: Keep some key verses in your mental pocket. When you feel anger rising, pull one out and focus on it.
- *Praise and Worship*: It's hard to stay angry when you're focusing on God's goodness. Try putting on some worship music when you feel your temperature rising.

Practical Techniques:

- *Deep Breathing:* Take a deep breath in for 4 counts, hold for 4, exhale for 4. Repeat until you feel calmer.
- *The 5-4-3-2-1 Grounding Technique:* Name 5 things you can see, 4 things you can touch, 3 things you can hear, 2 things you can smell, and 1 thing you can taste. This helps bring you back to the present moment.
- *The STOP Technique:* S - Stop what you're doing T - Take a breath O - Observe your thoughts and feelings P - Proceed with awareness

The spiritual practices focus on connecting with God and drawing strength from Him. They remind us of our identity in Christ and the bigger picture of God's plan. These can bring deep, lasting change as we allow God to work in our hearts.

The practical techniques, on the other hand, are more about managing our immediate physiological and psychological responses. They're like emergency brakes when we feel our emotions starting to run away with us.

The beauty is, we don't have to choose one or the other. We can and should use both! You might start with a practical technique to calm your immediate reaction, then move into prayer or scripture meditation for lasting peace and perspective.

Managing our physical state allows us to be in the right mind to make good decisions. We'll see how God supports our need for physical strength to fight spiritual battles in today's Biblical reading.

Which spiritual practice resonates with you the most? How might you incorporate it into your daily routine?

Of the practical techniques, which one do you think you're most likely to use? Why?

How do you think combining spiritual and practical techniques could enhance your ability to manage strong emotions?

READ 1 KINGS 19:1-18 (KJV)

After a great spiritual victory, Elijah found himself overcome by fear and despair. God's response included both practical care (rest and food) and spiritual renewal showing that we need a balance of both in life.

How did God address Elijah's physical needs before dealing with his spiritual state?

What spiritual practices did God use to restore Elijah's perspective and purpose?

How can Elijah's experience inform our approach to managing overwhelming emotions?

Today's Challenge

Choose one spiritual practice (Prayer, Scripture Meditation, or Praise and Worship) to focus on each day this week. Set three daily reminders on your phone to engage in your chosen practice. When you feel a strong emotion trying to board your bus, use the "1-2 Punch": Start with your most effective practical technique. Immediately follow it with your favorite spiritual practice. Note how this combined approach impacts your ability to manage the emotion.

What To Do Now

Log in to your member's area online so you can access this weeks group activity, discussion questions, and other resources to support your anger busting journey!

Get excited about next week because we'll explore real-life scenarios and develop strategies for applying the power of choice in our daily lives.

Remember, becoming emotionally and spiritually mature is a journey, not a destination. Some days you'll feel like you're walking on water, and other days you might feel like you're sinking. The important thing is that you're developing tools to help you stay afloat and keep your eyes on Jesus, no matter what waves come your way. You've got this, and more importantly, God's got you!

- **Day 1: Managing Expectations and Praying for Difficult People**
    - We learned about the gap between expectations and reality in challenging situations.
    - We explored the power of praying for those who frustrate or anger us.
    - We studied Jesus' teaching on loving our enemies (Matthew 5:43-45).
- **Day 2: The Heart Transformation and Emotional Control**
    - We discovered how consistent prayer can soften our hearts and change our perspective.
    - We explored bringing our emotions to God in prayer (Philippians 4:6-7).
- **Day 3: The Emotion Bus Route**
    - We learned about the "Emotion Bus" analogy and our role as the driver.
    - We explored how different emotions (passengers) can lead us to undesirable destinations.
- **Day 4: Combining Spiritual and Practical Techniques**
    - We discovered various spiritual practices and practical techniques for managing emotions.
    - We learned the importance of combining both approaches for effective emotional management.
    - We examined God's care for Elijah's physical and spiritual needs (1 Kings 19:1-18).

Week Four

A fool uttereth all his mind:
But a wise man keepeth it in till afterwards.
- Proverbs 29:11 (KJV)

Alright, folks, grab your hard hats because we're about to dive into a construction zone. Not the kind with orange cones and burly men holding "SLOW" signs, but the kind where God's trying to build something amazing in our lives, and we're sometimes our own wrecking ball. Let's meet our star builder (or should I say, *demolition expert*?), Jessica.

Before we dive too deep into Jessica's story, it's important to remember that while her anger outbursts may seem extreme, all expressions of anger - even subtle ones like the silent treatment or a scowl - can be harmful to our relationships with others and our walk with God. As you read, consider how your own expressions of anger, no matter how small they might seem, could be impacting your life and the lives of those around you.

Jessica was a force to be reckoned with. At 25, she had the ambition of a Silicon Valley CEO, the sass of a stand-up comedian, and unfortunately, the temper of a bull who just got a glimpse of red. Her friends often joked that her spirit animal was a porcupine – prickly on the outside, but undeniably cute if you could get past the quills.

Now, Jessica had dreams. Big dreams. She wanted to be a top-notch journalist, uncover corruption, give voice to the voiceless – you know, the whole superhero-with-a-pen package. She also had this secret Pinterest board full of wedding ideas, not that she'd ever admit it to anyone. But here's the kicker: Jessica's anger was like that one friend who always shows up uninvited to the party and manages to set something on fire.

Even in the best of circumstances, someway somehow, Jessica's emotions seemed to get the best of her. Often, before she even knew what had happened, she'd find herself yelling at the people around her, spewing her inner thoughts straight past that non-existent filter between her mouth and her brain.

The simplest of things would set her off. Maybe it would be someone cutting her off in traffic. Maybe it was that neighborhood kid that asked her the same question over and over again. And it wouldn't always be her spewing verbal vomit on innocent bystanders, sometimes it would just be the look of death that radiated from her eyes like superman's laser vision.

She always promised herself she'd try to do better, but deep down, she felt like what she was doing was enough. If people couldn't handle the heat, they should get out of the kitchen. But the reality is that Jessica had no idea how much her anger and lack of control was really costing her.

In what ways can you relate to Jessica? Have you ever felt like your own "wrecking ball" in situations where God might be trying to build something good?

How has anger affected your pursuit of your dreams or goals in the past?

If your friends were to describe your "spirit animal" based on how you handle anger, what would it be and why?

Bible Reading

READ NUMBERS 20:1-12 (KJV)

Moses, despite being described as very humble (Numbers 12:3), had a moment where his anger got the best of him, leading to serious consequences.

What factors do you think contributed to Moses' angry outburst?

How did Moses' action differ from what God instructed him to do?

What were the consequences of Moses' anger? How might this relate to how anger can impact our own lives and blessings?

Challenge

Review your anger journal. Imagine how each situation would have been different if you had responded with patience over of anger. Then, set one specific goal for how you want to handle anger differently in the coming week.

Remember...

Recognizing the impact of our anger is the first step towards change. You're not just avoiding negative consequences; you're opening the door for God's blessings. Keep at it – you're doing great work!

Wherefore, my beloved brethren, let every man be swift to hear, slow to speak, slow to wrath: for the wrath of man worketh not the righteousness of God. - James 1:19-20 (KJV)

One sunny Tuesday (because life-changing events always seem to happen on Tuesdays), God decided to play celestial matchmaker. He sent Jessica a young man named Michael, who was basically the human equivalent of a golden retriever – kind, loyal, and always happy to see you. Michael was an up-and-coming photojournalist, with a knack for capturing stories that made people's hearts grow three sizes, Grinch-style.

They met at a coffee shop (because where else do millennials meet?). Michael accidentally spilled his latte on Jessica's white blouse. Now, this could have been the start of a cute rom-com moment. But remember, Jessica's anger was always ready to RSVP to any event.

"Are you kidding me?" Jessica exploded, her voice reaching a decibel level usually reserved for rock concerts. "Do you just walk around looking for ways to ruin people's days, or am I just special?" Poor Michael stood there, a handful of napkins in his hand, looking like a puppy who'd just been caught chewing on a designer shoe. "I'm so sorry," he stammered. "Please, let me pay for the dry cleaning. And can I buy you a new coffee to make up for it?"

But Jessica was already storming out of the coffee shop, leaving Michael – and God's perfectly orchestrated meet-cute – in her wake.

A week later, God, being the persistent Heavenly Father He is, tried again to give Jessica what she'd been praying for. He arranged for Jessica to meet Olivia, the editor-in-chief of the exact type of hard-hitting news magazine Jessica dreamed of working for. They ended up sharing an Uber (because apparently, God's not above using ride-sharing apps for His divine purposes).

Olivia, impressed by Jessica's passionate chatter about investigative journalism, mentioned they had an opening for a junior reporter. Jessica's heart soared. This was it! Her big break!

But then, in true Jessica fashion, she noticed the driver taking a route she didn't agree with. "Hey," she snapped, leaning forward. "Are you trying to run up the fare? Don't you know how to do your job?" The driver, flustered, tried to explain about road work and detours, but Jessica was on a roll. She ranted about wasted time, her face flushed with anger.

Olivia sat quietly, observing. When they reached their destination, she turned to Jessica with a sympathetic smile. "You've got passion, that's for sure. But I think you might need a bit more... seasoning before you're ready for our team. Best of luck to you."

And just like that, another blessing slipped through Jessica's fingers, lost in the storm of her anger.

Can you recall a time when your anger caused you to miss out on a potential blessing or opportunity? How do you feel about it now?

How might Jessica's interactions with Michael and Olivia have gone differently if she had responded with patience instead of anger?

In what areas of your life do you find it most challenging to be slow to become angry? What are some things you can do starting right now to be slower to anger?

Bible Reading

READ 2 KINGS 5:1-14 (KJV)

Naaman almost missed out on healing because of his angry reaction to Elisha's simple instructions. Naaman's expectations were different from the reality of how God was using the situation to bless him. He almost missed his gift from God because of his own idea of how things should happen.

What aspects of Elisha's instructions angered Naaman? How might this relate to our own anger triggers?

How did Naaman's servants help him reconsider his angry response?

What blessings did Naaman receive when he finally set aside his anger and pride? How might this apply to our lives?

Keep In Mind...

God often works in mysterious ways. What looks like a coffee stain might just be the beginning of a beautiful story. By managing our anger and staying open to unexpected blessings, we position ourselves to receive the good things God has in store for us. Keep your eyes open and your temper in check – you never know what blessings are just around the corner!

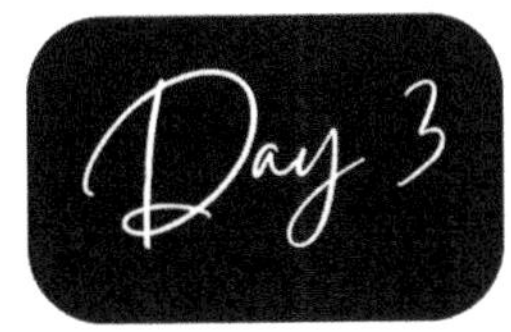

The discretion of a man deferreth his anger;
And it is his glory to pass over a transgression.
- Proverbs 19:11 (KJV)

It took a few more missed opportunities and a particularly disastrous family dinner (let's just say the turkey wasn't the only thing that got roasted) for Jessica to realize something needed to change. She was tired of feeling like a human tornado, leaving a trail of hurt feelings and missed chances in her wake.

That's when Jessica decided to take control of her anger instead of letting it control her. She started small – counting to ten before responding, going for a walk when she felt her temper rising, even trying out this weird thing called "prayer" that her grandma was always going on about.

Slowly but surely, things began to change. Jessica found herself pausing before reacting, choosing her words more carefully. She started seeing situations from other people's perspectives. And you know what? People started responding differently to her too.

Remember Michael, the latte spiller? Jessica ran into him again at a local art exhibit (God's timing is impeccable, isn't it?). This time, when he accidentally stepped on her toe, Jessica took a deep breath and said, "No worries! These shoes have been through worse."

They got to talking, and wouldn't you know it, they hit it off. Turns out, Michael's clumsiness was balanced out by his wit, kindness, and ability to capture the most amazing photos.

And Olivia? Well, Jessica's path crossed with hers again at a journalism conference. This time, when a speaker said something Jessica vehemently disagreed with, instead of causing a scene, she engaged in a respectful debate afterwards.

Olivia noticed, remembering the fiery young woman from the Uber. She was impressed by Jessica's growth and offered her an internship on the spot.

As Jessica's anger subsided, it was like the fog cleared, revealing all the blessings God had been trying to send her way. A fulfilling career, a loving relationship, stronger friendships – all the things that had seemed out of reach were suddenly within her grasp.

Can you identify a "turning point" in your own life where you realized your anger was costing you too much? What led to this realization?

Which of Jessica's small steps towards managing her anger resonates most with you? Why?

Have you ever had a "redemption run-in" – a second chance to make a better impression or handle a situation more positively? How did it go?

Bible Reading

READ GENESIS 45:1-15 (KJV)

Joseph, after years of separation and potential for bitter anger, chooses forgiveness and reconciliation when he meets his brothers again.

How do you think Joseph managed his anger and hurt over the years?

What blessings came as a result of Joseph's choice to forgive rather than seek revenge?

How might Joseph's story inspire us in dealing with long-standing hurts or resentments in our own lives?

Challenge

Make a list of 5 areas in your life where you've struggled with anger in the past (e.g., work, family, traffic, etc.). For each area, set an intention to look for one blessing or positive aspect today. As you go through your day, actively search for these blessings. They might be small (like a coworker's kind word) or large (like a new opportunity). When you spot a blessing, write it down and take a moment to thank God for it. At the end of the day, reflect on your findings. How did actively looking for blessings change your perspective and your reactions throughout the day?

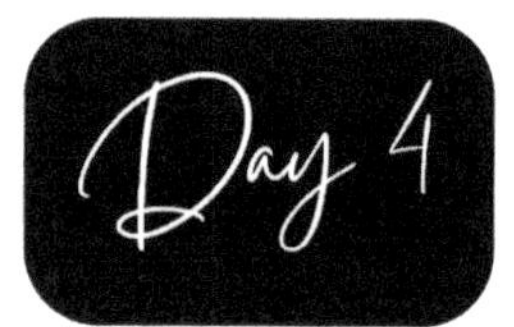

Be not hasty in thy spirit to be angry: for anger resteth in the bosom of fools. - Ecclesiastes 7:9 (KJV)

Let's take a moment to chat about why God cares so much about us managing our anger. It's not because He's a cosmic killjoy who doesn't want us to express our emotions. Nope, it's because He loves us more than we can imagine and doesn't want us to hurt ourselves or others.

Think of it this way: when a parent tells their toddler not to touch the hot stove, it's not because they're trying to ruin the kid's fun. It's because they know that touching that stove is going to result in pain and tears and possibly a trip to the ER. God's commands about controlling our anger are like that – they're not restrictions, they're protection.

Now, let's get practical. We've talked about how anger can derail us from God's blessings, but how do we actually deal with it in the moment? Imagine anger as a train. The longer you ride it, the further it takes you from your destination (you know, that place where all God's blessings are waiting for you).

Here are some signs you might be boarding the anger train:

1. Your heart starts racing faster than a caffeinated chipmunk.
2. Your thoughts start spiraling into worst-case scenarios.
3. You have a sudden urge to say something sarcastic (and not the fun kind of sarcastic).
4. Your body tenses up like you're preparing for a boxing match with life itself.
5. You start seeing red, and not because you're at a bullfighting convention.

If you notice these signs, congratulations! Your self-awareness just leveled up. Now, here's how you can get off that train before it leaves the station:

- **The Emergency Brake** (Deep Breathing): Take a deep breath in for 4 counts, hold for 4, out for 4. Repeat until you no longer feel the need to breathe fire like a dragon. Remember, you can't deep breathe and talk at the same time so make sure to keep your mouth shut.
- **The Scenic Route** (Reframing): Ask yourself, "Will this matter in 5 years?" If not, maybe it's not worth getting your knickers in a twist over.
- **The Station Swap** (Change Your Environment): If possible, physically remove yourself from the situation. Go for a walk, or at least to the bathroom. A change of scenery can be like a reset button for your emotions.
- **The Conductor's Announcement** (Self-Talk): Remind yourself, "I am in control of my reactions." You're the conductor of your emotional train, not a helpless passenger.
- **The Divine Intervention** (Prayer): Send up a quick SOS to the Big Guy upstairs. Something like, "God, I could really use some of that patience fruit right about now!"

How does viewing God's commands about anger as protection rather than restriction change your perspective?

Which of the signs of boarding the anger train do you most often experience?

Of the techniques for getting off the anger train, which one do you think would be most effective for you? Why? How can you start implementing this today?

Bible Reading

READ JOHN 2:13-17 (KJV)

Jesus, upon finding the temple courts filled with merchants, expresses what many call "righteous anger."

How does Jesus' anger in this situation differ from the destructive anger we often experience?

What was the motivation behind Jesus' actions? How does this compare to our usual motivations when we're angry?

How did Jesus' actions in the temple ultimately serve God's purposes? What can we learn from this about the proper use of strong emotions?

Today's Challenge

Create your own "Anger Train Emergency Kit." On a small card or in a note on your phone, write down: 5 signs you're boarding the anger train, 5 techniques for getting off the train, a short, meaningful Bible verse about peace or self-control. Keep this "emergency kit" with you at all times. Use it when you feel yourself boarding the anger train.

Food For Thought...

Remember, the goal isn't to never feel angry. Anger is a normal human emotion. The goal is to manage it so it doesn't hijack your life and drive you miles away from where God wants you to be. By learning to recognize the signs of anger and having tools ready to manage it, you're positioning yourself to receive the blessings God has in store for you. You're not just avoiding negative consequences; you're actively creating space for peace, joy, and love in your life. Keep up the great work – you're on the right track!

As we wrap up this chapter, I want to leave you with this thought: God's blessings are like Amazon Prime – they're ready to be delivered to you at any moment. But if anger is always answering the door, those blessings might just get returned to sender. So let's work on making sure love, joy, peace, and all their cool friends are the ones greeting the delivery guy, okay?

In the next chapter, we'll dive deeper into practical strategies for not just managing anger, but replacing it with the kind of godly responses that roll out the red carpet for blessings. Until then, remember: God's love for you is bigger than your biggest angry outburst, and His grace is more powerful than your strongest emotion. Even if that emotion is currently telling you to flip a table. (*Seriously, don't flip the table. It never ends well, and tables are expensive.*)

Make sure to login to your account at www.youarenotcalled.com to get this weeks resources!

Weekly Recap

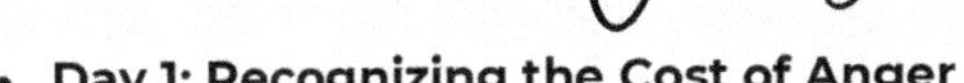

- **Day 1: Recognizing the Cost of Anger**
  - We met Jessica and explored how anger can be our own "wrecking ball" in life.
- **Day 2: Missed Opportunities and Second Chances**
  - We explored Naaman's story and how anger can blind us to blessings.
  - We practiced the "Blessing in Disguise" technique to reframe frustrating situations.
- **Day 3: The Turning Point and Redemption**
  - We saw Jessica's journey of change and her "redemption run-ins" with Michael and Olivia.
  - We studied Joseph's story of forgiveness and how it led to blessings.
  - We went on an adventure to actively look for positives in our lives.
- **Day 4: God's Protection and Getting Off the Anger Train**
  - We understood God's guidance on anger as protection, not restriction.
  - We learned about the "Anger Train" analogy and techniques to "get off the train."
  - We examined Jesus' righteous anger in the temple and created our "Anger Train Emergency Kit."

Week Five

And we know that all things work together for good to them that love God, to them who are the called according to his purpose.
- Romans 8:28 (KJV)

[Content warning: This chapter contains references to childhood trauma and SA.]

The summer I turned twelve was supposed to be filled with the carefree joy of childhood. Instead, it became the summer that changed everything.

I remember that night vividly - the kind of sweltering Southern afternoon where the air feels thick enough to cut with a knife. My grandmother and I had driven an hour south to visit family we hadn't seen in what felt like forever. The excitement bubbled in my chest as we pulled up to the house, my eyes scanning for my cousins.

When my oldest cousin suggested we go for a walk, my heart soared. He was the cool one, you know? Always hanging out with the older kids, barely sparing a glance for his kid cousin. But here he was, inviting me along. Me! I felt like I'd just been handed a golden ticket to the land of Grown-Up Cool.

We set off down the street, the cicadas providing a pulsing backdrop to our adventure. As we wove between houses, leaving the watchful eyes of adults behind, I couldn't help but feel a thrill of independence. This was what being grown-up felt like, right? I had no idea I was walking towards a moment that would change me forever when he took something from me that I could never get back.

Living in a Fallen World

The painful experience shared above is a stark reminder that we live in a fallen world. A world where innocence can be shattered in an instant, where trust can be betrayed, and where the actions of others can leave deep, lasting scars on our hearts and minds.

It's natural to question why such things happen, to wonder where God is in the midst of our pain. We might find ourselves asking, "If God is good, why does He allow such suffering?" These are not easy questions, and the answers are not always clear or satisfying in the moment.

Yet, even in our darkest hours, we cling to the promise in Romans 8:28. This verse doesn't say that all things are good, but that God works all things for the good of those who love Him. It's a promise that even in our pain, even in the midst of terrible injustice, God is at work, weaving a tapestry of redemption that we may not be able to see clearly in the moment.

Bible Reading

READ JOB 42:12-17 (KJV)

The story of Job provides a powerful illustration of confronting immense pain while holding onto faith in God's ultimate goodness. Job was a righteous man who experienced devastating loss - his wealth, his children, and his health were all stripped away. His suffering was so great that even his wife advised him to "curse God and die" (Job 2:9).

Throughout his ordeal, Job wrestled with difficult questions about why he was suffering. His friends offered simplistic explanations that only added to his pain. Yet, even in his darkest moments, Job clung to his faith in God's character.

In the end, God spoke to Job out of a whirlwind (Job 38-41). While God didn't provide a direct explanation for Job's suffering, He reminded Job of His power, wisdom, and sovereignty over all creation. Job's response is profound: "My ears had heard of you but now my eyes have seen you" (Job 42:5).

God then restored Job's fortunes, giving him twice as much as he had before. This doesn't erase the pain Job experienced, but it demonstrates God's ability to bring good out of even the most terrible circumstances.

Have you ever experienced a time when you felt God was absent or questioned His goodness? How did you navigate through those feelings?

In what ways can you relate to Job's experience of suffering and questioning?

Challenge

Today's challenge is to take a courageous step in confronting areas of pain in your life.

1. Find a quiet place where you can be alone with God.
2. In a journal or on a piece of paper, write down areas of hurt, pain, or injustice in your life that you've been struggling to understand or accept.
3. For each item you've written, try to express your honest feelings to God about it. It's okay to express anger, confusion, or doubt - God can handle your raw emotions.
4. After you've expressed your feelings, write the words of Romans 8:28 next to each item.
5. Spend a few moments in prayer, asking God to help you trust in His promise to work all things for good, even when you can't see or understand how.

Remember...

Confronting our pain is not about minimizing it or pretending it doesn't hurt. It's about bringing our whole selves - including our wounds - before God, trusting that He is big enough to handle our pain and loving enough to work through it for our ultimate good.

As we continue this chapter, we'll explore how God's grace and the practice of forgiveness can be powerful tools in our journey of healing and restoration. Even when the path seems twisted and dark, God is with you, working all things for your good.

If you're holding onto something deep or are struggling in a particular area, remember there is support out there in the form of therapists and physicians. Don't be afraid to get the help you need to support your journey.

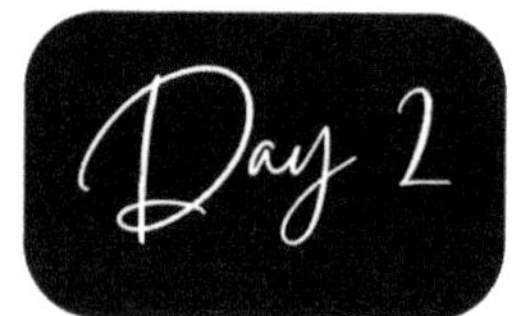

For by grace are ye saved through faith; and that not of yourselves: it is the gift of God. - Ephesians 2:8 (KJV)

As we continue our journey through this challenging topic, let's take a moment to explore a concept that has the power to transform even our deepest wounds: grace.

What happened on that twisted path shaped most of my life on this planet. For years the impact of that event left me angry and questioning my worth and value. For far too long, I believed that what happened was my fault.

The weight of this misconception was heavy, influencing every aspect of my life. It colored my perceptions, tainted my relationships, and cast a long shadow over my sense of self. I carried this burden silently, letting it shape my world in ways I didn't fully comprehend.

But here's where grace enters the picture. Grace is God's unmerited favor. It's like winning the cosmic lottery, except you didn't even buy a ticket. Grace is God looking at us – messy, complicated, often-stubborn us – and saying, "You know what? I love you anyway, and I'm going to help you out."

The Bible is full of examples of God's grace in action:

Noah: God looked at a world full of wickedness and chose to save Noah and his family. Noah didn't earn this; it was pure grace.

Moses: Despite his anger issues and initial reluctance, God chose Moses to lead His people out of Egypt.

David: Even after committing adultery and murder, David was still called a man after God's own heart.

These stories remind us that God's grace isn't dependent on our perfection or even our ability to have it all together. It's freely given, even when we feel unworthy or broken.

No matter what you've done, no matter what you've been through, the God of the universe loves you and will show you grace through all the impossible situations when you hand them over to him.

How do you define grace? How does the concept of grace challenge your view of God?

Can you identify moments in your life where you've experienced God's grace? Are there any areas in your life that you still need to accept God's grace?

How might embracing God's grace change how you view yourself and your past?

Bible Reading

READ 2 CORINTHIANS 12: 9-10
& HEBREWS 4:16 (KJV)

God's grace is more than enough to cover our shortcomings and struggles. In fact, it's in our moments of weakness that God's strength shines brightest. So, let's boldly approach God's throne of grace, accepting His help in our times of need, knowing that our weaknesses are opportunities for His power to be displayed in our lives.

What does it mean to delight in weaknesses and difficulties? Do you think this is something that you are doing in your life?

What are some weaknesses in your life that God could be strong in?

Do you approach God's throne of grace with confidence? How could you begin doing this?

Keep In Mind...

Remember, God's grace is big enough to cover every hurt, every mistake, every "unforgivable" act. As we continue to explore this journey of healing, let's hold onto the truth that we are deeply loved and infinitely valued by a God of limitless grace.

And when ye stand praying, forgive, if ye have ought against any: that your Father also which is in heaven may forgive you your trespasses.
- Mark 11:25 (KJV)

Only when I grew up and could see things from an adult perspective did I understand how wrong what happened to me was. This realization, while liberating in some ways, initially fueled even more anger. The injustice of it all, the stolen innocence, the years lost to misplaced guilt – it was overwhelming.

This anger became a constant companion, an invisible barrier that affected all of my relationships. It was like a wall I had built around myself, ostensibly for protection, but in reality, it was keeping out love and connection as much as it was keeping out potential hurt.

Forgiveness, especially when the hurt runs deep, can feel about as appealing as a root canal performed by a blindfolded dentist. But remember – forgiveness isn't about the other person. It's about you.

Forgiveness doesn't mean what they did was okay. It doesn't mean you have to be best buddies with them or even have them in your life at all. Forgiveness is about releasing the hold that person and that hurt have on you. It's about choosing to lay down the heavy backpack of anger and resentment you've been lugging around.

Let's look at some practical steps towards forgiveness:

- **Make it a daily choice:** Forgiveness isn't a one-and-done deal. It's a choice you might have to make every single day.
- **Pray for the person:** This sounds challenging, but praying for someone who hurt you can soften your heart over time.
- **Reframe the situation:** Try to see the bigger picture. The person who hurt you is also a flawed human being, probably acting out of their own pain or ignorance.

Are there any people or situations that you avoid thinking about or discussing? What emotions come up when you do consider them?

If you could go back in time and change one painful event in your life, what would it be? How has this event affected your ability to trust or connect with others?

Imagine extending forgiveness to the person who hurt you. What fears or reservations come up? How might your life change if you were able to release this anger and hurt?

Bible Reading

READ LUKE 23:34 (KJV)

Perhaps the most powerful example of forgiveness in the Bible is Jesus on the cross. Even in His moment of greatest suffering, Jesus chose forgiveness. This doesn't mean what was done to Him was okay. It doesn't minimize His pain. But it does show us the power of choosing forgiveness even in the face of great injustice.

Jesus forgave those who were actively crucifying Him. How does this challenge your own limits of forgiveness?

In saying "Father, forgive them, for they do not know what they are doing," Jesus acknowledged the ignorance of His persecutors. How might understanding the limited perspective of those who hurt you affect your ability to forgive them?

Jesus' act of forgiveness on the cross was a pivotal moment in human history. How might your decision to forgive, even in extremely difficult circumstances, impact your life and the lives of those around you?

Challenge

Identify someone who has hurt you that you're struggling to forgive. Set a timer for 2 minutes. Spend that time sincerely praying for that person's well-being. After the timer goes off, journal about how you feel. Repeat this exercise daily for a week, noting any changes in your feelings or perspective.

Forbearing one another, and forgiving one another, if any man have a quarrel against any: even as Christ forgave you, so also do ye. - Colossians 3:13 (KJV)

It took God's grace and my journey of learning forgiveness to break down the barrier of anger I had built. The process wasn't easy or quick. It required facing painful truths, challenging long-held beliefs, and making the difficult choice to forgive – not just once, but over and over again.

If this journey into forgiveness is harder than you feel like it should be, you're not alone. I've had the distinct privilege of working with women around the world. What I've found is that this is the one area that we all struggle in.

The older we get, the more we realize how wrong injustices that happened to us were. But we have the choice to let it go and release ourselves from the bondage of anger and bitterness.

For me, this journey of forgiveness didn't erase what happened, but it did start to loosen the grip that event had on my life. It opened the door to healing, to reclaiming my worth, and to forming deeper, more authentic connections with my loved ones.

Choosing forgiveness daily isn't always easy, but it's always worth it. Here are some additional strategies to help make forgiveness a regular part of your life:

- *Practice empathy:* Try to understand the other person's perspective, even if you don't agree with their actions.
- *Choose to release anger:* When angry feelings bubble up, visualize them as a balloon floating away. Don't let that dark feeling come in and control you.
- *Seek professional help:* Sometimes, the hurt is too deep to navigate alone. There's no shame in talking to a therapist or counselor.
- *Surround yourself with Christian friends:* Not everyone realizes the impact that forgiveness has on our own lives and the lives of others. Surrounding yourself with those people who share your morals and values will give you a support system when you need it. Make sure these people are ones who can be present for your big emotions without judgement. You deserve a safe space to rest while you walk through this journey of forgiveness.

Bible Reading

READ LUKE 15:11-32 (KJV)

The father in the story doesn't wait for his son to grovel or make amends. Instead, he runs to meet him, embraces him, and celebrates his return.
This story challenges us to consider: Can we extend this kind of gracious, preemptive forgiveness to others? Can we forgive before the other person asks for it?

How has your understanding of forgiveness evolved throughout this study?

In what ways have you experienced healing through extending or receiving forgiveness?

What's one step you can take today to make forgiveness a more regular part of your life?

Remember...

God's love for you is bigger than your biggest hurt, and His grace is more powerful than your deepest pain. Even when forgiveness feels impossible, remember that with God, all things are possible. You are on a journey of healing and growth, and every step forward, no matter how small, is a victory worth celebrating.

What's Next

As we move forward, we'll be exploring how to apply the principles of grace and forgiveness in our daily lives and relationships. In the next chapter, "Living Out Grace and Forgiveness," we'll dive into practical scenarios and develop strategies for:

- Extending grace in challenging relationships
- Setting healthy boundaries while practicing forgiveness
- Dealing with recurring hurts and the challenge of forgiving repeatedly
- Applying grace and forgiveness in various contexts (family, work, church, etc.)

Remember, the journey of grace and forgiveness is ongoing. There will be challenges along the way, but each step you take brings you closer to the freedom and peace God desires for you. Keep pressing on. The best is yet to come!

Make sure to login to your account at youarenotcalled.com to get this weeks resources!

- **Day 1: Confronting Our Pain**
  - We explored the reality of living in a fallen world and God's promise to work all things for good (Romans 8:28).
  - We learned from Job's story about maintaining faith in the midst of suffering.
- **Day 2: Understanding God's Grace**
  - We defined grace as God's unmerited favor.
  - We examined biblical examples of grace (Noah, Moses, David).
  - We practiced recognizing daily instances of grace in our lives.
- **Day 3: The Journey to Forgiveness**
  - We explored forgiveness as a process of releasing others and ourselves.
  - We learned practical steps towards forgiveness.
  - We reflected on Jesus' example of forgiveness on the cross.
- **Day 4: Choosing Forgiveness Daily**
  - We discovered how daily forgiveness can lead to healing and deeper relationships.
  - We examined additional strategies for making forgiveness a regular practice.
  - We considered the parable of the Prodigal Son as an example of preemptive forgiveness.

Week Six

Charity suffereth long, and is kind; charity envieth not; charity vaunteth not itself, is not puffed up, 5doth not behave itself unseemly, seeketh not her own, is not easily provoked, thinketh no evil.
- 1 Corinthians 13:4-5 (KJV)

Grab your favorite fuzzy blanket and a cup of hot cocoa, because we're about to dive into the warm and fuzzies. That's right, we're talking about love! Not the Hollywood, rom-com kind of love (although those are fun too), but the deep, transformative, anger-dissolving kind of love that changes lives.

Let's kick things off with a story that'll make your heart grow three sizes, Grinch-style.

Meet Sarah, a foster mom with a heart of gold and the patience of a saint (most days, anyway). Sarah had fostered many children over the years, but none quite like Max. At 12 years old, Max was a tornado of anger and hurt, lashing out at anyone who dared to get close. His file was thicker than a New York phone book, filled with incidents of aggression, property damage, and colorful language that would make a sailor blush.

Most foster families had given up on Max within weeks. But Sarah? She was made of sterner stuff. From day one, she met Max's anger with unwavering love and kindness. When he yelled, she spoke softly. When he broke things, she helped him clean up without judgment. When he pushed her away, she simply said, "I'm not going anywhere, kiddo."

Months passed, and Max's outbursts slowly began to decrease. One day, after a particularly rough day at school, Max came home and, instead of slamming doors, he asked Sarah for a hug. As she held him, feeling his small frame shake with sobs, Max whispered, "Why haven't you given up on me like everyone else?"

Sarah's answer was simple: "Because love doesn't give up, Max. And I love you, no matter what."

That moment was a turning point for Max. He'd finally encountered a love that was truly unconditional, a love that saw past his anger to the hurt child underneath. Over time, Max's anger began to melt away, replaced by a growing sense of security and self-worth.

Years later, when Max graduated high school (with honors, I might add), he dedicated his achievement to Sarah. "She loved me when I was unlovable," he said, "and that love changed everything."

Now, if that story didn't give you warm fuzzies, you might want to check if you've accidentally swapped your heart for a potato. But here's the kicker - this kind of transformative love isn't just the stuff of heartwarming stories. It's actually what Christ does for us and what we're called to as followers of Christ.

How does Sarah's unwavering love for Max, despite his challenging behavior, mirror God's unconditional love for us? Can you think of a time when you experienced or witnessed this kind of persistent love?

Max's behavior changed over time in response to Sarah's consistent love. How might consistently choosing to respond with love, even in difficult situations, transform your relationships or environment?

Sarah saw past Max's anger to the hurt child underneath. How can developing this perspective help you respond with love to difficult people in your life? Is there someone in your life right now who might need this kind of understanding?

Bible Reading

READ 1 PETER 4:8 &
1 CORINTHIANS 13:4-5 (KJV)

By embracing and embodying this kind of love, we not only reflect God's character but also create an environment where forgiveness, grace, and healing can flourish, ultimately leading to deeper, more meaningful connections with both God and others.

How has God's love "covered a multitude of sins" in your own life? How might this perspective change the way you view and interact with others who have wronged you?

1 Corinthians 13:5 says that love "keeps no record of wrongs." In what areas of your life do you find yourself holding onto past hurts or offenses? How could letting go of these "records" transform your relationships?

Reflecting on the qualities of love described in 1 Corinthians 13:4-5 (patient, kind, not envious, not boastful, not proud, not dishonoring others, not self-seeking, not easily angered), which aspect do you find most challenging to embody? How might focusing on developing this quality impact your ability to love others more fully?

Challenge

For the next week, commit to practicing "love that covers" in your daily interactions. Each day, choose one person (especially someone you find challenging) and consciously embody one aspect of love from 1 Corinthians 13:4-5 towards them. At the end of each day, reflect on how this intentional love affected your interactions and attitude.

O Jerusalem, Jerusalem, thou that killest the prophets, and stonest them which are sent unto thee, how often would I have gathered thy children together, even as a hen gathereth her chickens under her wings, and ye would not! Behold, your house is left unto you desolate. For I say unto you, Ye shall not see me henceforth, till ye shall say, Blessed is he that cometh in the name of the Lord.
- Matthew 22:37-39 (KJV)

Jesus emphasized love so much that He said it was the greatest commandment. When asked about the most important commandment, Jesus replied, "Love the Lord your God with all your heart and with all your soul and with all your mind. This is the first and greatest commandment. And the second is like it: Love your neighbor as yourself" (Matthew 22:37-39).

Notice how Jesus sneaks in that bit about loving yourself? That's not an accident, folks. Which brings us to our next point: loving ourselves.

Now, I know what some of you are thinking. "Love myself? But I'm a hot mess! I've got more issues than a magazine stand." Well, buckle up, buttercup, because we're about to go on a self-love journey.

Meet Tom. Tom was the kind of guy who could find fault in a perfect sunset. He'd messed up big time in his past - failed businesses, broken relationships, the works. He walked around with a cloud of self-loathing so thick you could practically see it.

One day, Tom's pastor challenged him to look in the mirror every morning and say one kind thing to himself. Tom thought it was the dumbest idea he'd ever heard (and he'd heard some doozies). But, being a good sport, he decided to give it a shot.

The first morning, Tom stared at his reflection and managed a grudging, "Your... uh... eyebrows are symmetrical. Good job." It felt ridiculous, but he kept at it. Day by day, the compliments got a little easier, a little more genuine.

"You're trying your best." "You're a good friend." "You're forgiven and loved by God."

Slowly but surely, Tom's perspective began to shift. He started to see himself through God's eyes - as a beloved child, worthy of love and forgiveness. And you know what? As Tom learned to love and forgive himself, he found it easier to love and forgive others too.

How do you think your ability to love others is affected by how you view and treat yourself? Can you recall a time when your self-perception influenced your interactions with others?

Jesus commands us to love our neighbors as ourselves. In what areas of your life do you find it challenging to extend the same grace and forgiveness to yourself that you offer to others?

Tom's journey of self-love began with small, daily affirmations. What is one positive truth about yourself that you could start affirming daily, and how might this practice change your overall self-perception over time?

Bible Reading

READ PSALM 139:13-14 (KJV)

David's confidence in God's love for him wasn't based on his perfect behavior (hello, Bathsheba scandal), but on his understanding of God's character and his identity as God's creation. He was able to forgive himself because God forgave him.

Do you love yourself the way that God loves you? How do you think your life would be different if you truly loved yourself in that way?

In what areas of your life do you struggle to accept or love yourself? How might viewing these aspects through God's eyes of love change your perspective?

Can you list three unique qualities or talents you possess that reflect God's creativity and care in making you? How can you celebrate these aspects of yourself more fully?

Challenge

Find a quiet place where you won't be interrupted. Take a deep breath and ask God to help you see yourself through His eyes. Write a letter to yourself, focusing on your positive qualities, your achievements (big and small), and the unique ways God has gifted you. Include words of forgiveness for past mistakes and encouragement for your future. End the letter with a reminder of God's unconditional love for you. Seal the letter and keep it somewhere safe. Open and read it whenever you need a boost.

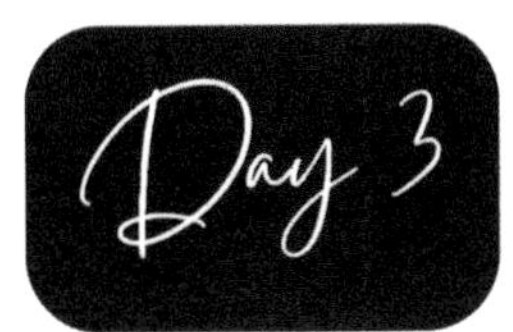

For if ye love them which love you, what reward have ye? do not even the publicans the same?
- Matthew 5:46 (KJV)

Let's be real - some people make it really hard to love them. They're like human versions of those prickly burrs that stick to your socks on a nature hike.

Meet Linda. Linda had a coworker, Karen (yes, that Karen), who was the human equivalent of nails on a chalkboard. Karen criticized everything Linda did, took credit for Linda's ideas, and had a laugh that could curdle milk.

Linda's first instinct was to fight fire with fire. She fantasized about putting laxatives in Karen's coffee or "accidentally" deleting all her files. But then Linda remembered the whole "love your enemies" thing. Ugh.

So, Linda decided to try a radical experiment: she would treat Karen with kindness, no matter what. She complimented Karen's ideas (even the not-so-great ones), offered to help with projects, and even brought her favorite coffee one morning.

At first, Karen was suspicious. Was Linda trying to poison her?

But as days turned into weeks, something shifted. Karen's criticisms became less frequent, her laugh a little less grating. One day, she even thanked Linda for her help on a project.

They never became best friends, but the office atmosphere improved dramatically.

And Linda? She found that choosing love over anger left her feeling lighter, happier, and more at peace.

Can you think of a few people who are tough to love that you interact with often? What are some ways that you are maybe not so loving right now?

What actions could you take to be more loving in these relationships and to find more peace with these people?

What would be a barrier that might keep you from being more loving and showing grace to these people? How can you overcome that barrier?

Bible Reading

READ ACTS 7:54-60 (KJV)

Stephen's example shows us that loving our enemies isn't about warm fuzzy feelings. It's a choice we make, even in the face of hostility and injustice. It's about breaking the cycle of anger and retaliation, just as Christ did. If Stephen, a mere human like us, was able to show forgiveness in this awful situation, can't we forgive that lunatic that cut us off in traffic?

Can you recall a time when choosing love over anger changed a situation for the better?

What makes loving your "enemies" so challenging? How might this challenge actually be an opportunity for spiritual growth?

How does Stephen's example challenge or inspire you in dealing with those who hurt you?

Challenge

For the next week, commit to the Kindness Challenge: Identify someone in your life who's difficult to love (your "Karen"). Each day, do one intentional act of kindness for this person. It could be as simple as a genuine compliment, offering help with a task, or bringing them their favorite snack. If negative thoughts arise, pause and pray for the person instead. Keep a journal of your experiences. Note any changes in the person's behavior, but more importantly, note any changes in your own heart and mindset. At the end of the week, reflect on how this challenge impacted you and your relationship with this person.

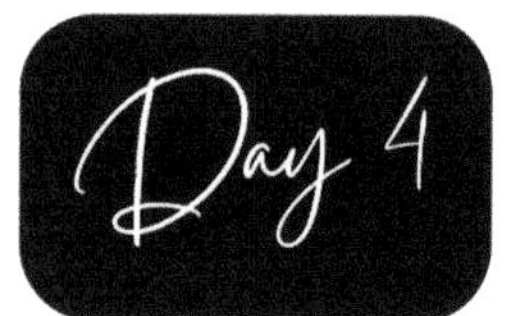

Keep thy heart with all diligence;
For out of it are the issues of life.
- Proverbs 4:23 (KJV)

Now, listen sis, not only do we have to love ourselves and love others and love God, we also have to teach other people how to love us. Crazy right? The wildest thing I ever realized in my life is that I was already teaching other people how to love me.

If you don't remember anything else from this book, remember this: **you teach people how to treat you by how you treat yourself.**

If you disrespect yourself, other people feel they can disrespect you too. If you don't hold true to the promises you make to yourself, other people feel that they didn't have to hold their promises to you either. *You are the first example that others see in what you expect and what you will tolerate.*

We are the only example that other people have in how to love us. We teach people how to love us by first loving ourselves. It's like being the instructor in a "How to Love [Your Name]" class.

Meet Alex. Alex had always struggled with feeling unworthy of love. She bent over backwards to please others, never voiced her own needs, and accepted scraps of affection as if they were five-course meals.

One day, after yet another disappointing relationship, Alex had an epiphany. She realized that by not valuing herself, she was teaching others not to value her either. It was time for a change.

Alex started small. She began saying no to things she didn't want to do. She voiced her opinions, even when they differed from others. She asked for what she needed in relationships. At first, it felt uncomfortable, even selfish. But Alex kept reminding herself: "I am worthy of love and respect."

To her surprise, people responded positively. Sure, some folks who were used to walking all over her were a bit miffed at first. But genuine friends and potential partners appreciated the more authentic Alex. By loving herself more, Alex was teaching others how to truly love her too.

Next week, we're going to dive deep into loving ourselves and how to teach others how to love us through boundary setting and our own example. For today, let's dip our toes into the water of boundaries and how our actions impact how others treat us.

Have you ever thought about the way you treat yourself being a guide to others as to how to treat you? In what ways have you seen this truth play out in your life?

What have you taught others about how to treat you this far in your life? Are there any boundaries that you need to set with the people around you?

How might you want to re-educate those around you? What steps will you take now to start retraining those around you in how to love you properly?

Bible Reading

READ MARK 1:35-39 (KJV)

Even Jesus, the epitome of love, set boundaries. We see Jesus withdrawing to a quiet place to pray, despite the demands of the crowd. When His disciples find Him, saying everyone is looking for Him, Jesus doesn't immediately rush back. Instead, He decides it's time to move on to other villages.

This shows us that setting boundaries isn't selfish - it's necessary for maintaining our well-being and fulfilling our purpose. Jesus modeled that it's okay to say no, to take time for spiritual renewal, and to not be at everyone's beck and call.

In what areas of your life do you need to establish better boundaries?

Can you think of a time when setting a boundary improved a relationship? How did it feel?

How might your relationships change if you consistently chose to keep your peace by establishing healthy boundaries?

Today's Challenge

Take some time to ask yourself, "When am I saying yes when I really want to say no and when am I saying no when I really want to say yes?" Maybe this means saying yes to additional activities when you know your schedule is already full. Maybe this means saying no when you really want to go back to school because you think it won't work out or it will put too much of a burden on others. Maybe it's something else entirely, but either way, ask yourself the question so you can identify where you need to do some work on your own boundaries.

What's Next...

Remember, setting boundaries is an act of love - both for yourself and for others. It's about teaching people how to treat you with respect and dignity, just as God treats you.

As we wrap up this chapter, remember that love - for God, for yourself, and for others - is the foundation of everything. It's the antidote to anger, the balm for hurt, and the key to living out God's purpose for your life.

Will it always be easy? Nope. There will be days when you want to trade all this love stuff for a good old-fashioned anger fest. But stick with it. Choose love, again and again. Because where love abounds, anger cannot exist.

As we move forward, we'll be exploring how to maintain this love-centered approach to life in a world that often seems determined to push our buttons. In the next chapter, we'll dive into strategies for choosing love in high-stress situations, how to love yourself during times of failure or disappointment, practical ways to show love to difficult people without compromising your boundaries, and how to maintain a love-first mindset in a sometimes hostile world.

Make sure to login to your account at youarenotcalled.com to get this weeks resources!

- **Day 1: The Transformative Power of Unconditional Love**
  - We explored Sarah and Max's story, illustrating how unconditional love can transform lives.
  - We learned about Jesus' example of love on the cross (Luke 23:34).
  - We practiced the Mirror Exercise to cultivate self-love and positive self-talk.
- **Day 2: Loving Yourself as God Loves You**
  - We discovered Tom's journey to self-love through daily affirmations.
  - We examined David's confidence in God's love (Psalm 139:13-14).
  - We wrote love letters to ourselves as an act of self-compassion.
- **Day 3: Loving Others, Even When It's Difficult**
  - We witnessed Linda's experiment in loving her difficult coworker, Karen.
  - We learned from Stephen's example of forgiving his persecutors (Acts 7:54-60).
  - We took on the Kindness Challenge to practice loving difficult people.
- **Day 4: Teaching Others How to Love Us**
  - We followed Alex's journey in setting healthy boundaries.
  - We observed Jesus setting boundaries in His ministry (Mark 1:35-39).
  - We created a Boundaries Blueprint to implement in our own lives.

Week Seven

But let your communication be, Yea, yea; Nay, nay: for whatsoever is more than these cometh of evil.
- Matthew 5:37 (KJV)

Alright, folks, grab your metaphorical safety goggles, because we're about to do some serious boundary building! Don't worry, it's not as complicated as assembling IKEA furniture (thank heavens), but it might just revolutionize your life. Ready? Let's dive in!

Picture this: There I was, a fresh-faced business owner with stars in my eyes and the stamina of a caffeinated squirrel. My business motto? "Yes is best!" I was like a puppy at a treat factory, eagerly wagging my tail at every opportunity that came my way. New client? Yes! Last-minute project? Absolutely! Work through the weekend? Why not! I was living the dream... or so I thought.

Fast forward a few months, and I was less "bright-eyed and bushy-tailed" and more "bloodshot-eyed and frazzled-tailed." I had taken on clients who were more high-maintenance than a poodle with a tiara. I was working hours that would make an owl say, "Whoa, take a break!" And my family? They were starting to forget what I looked like without a laptop attached to my hands.

The worst part? I was becoming the very thing I started my business to avoid - a stressed-out, resentful grouch who couldn't enjoy the fruits of her labor. My clients were starting to feel less like opportunities and more like burdens. My once-beloved business was turning into a source of frustration. And let's not even talk about my "stellar" performance as a wife, mother, and follower of Christ. (Spoiler alert: it wasn't stellar. It wasn't even in the same galaxy as stellar.)

That's when it hit me like a ton of bricks (or a particularly heavy laptop): every "yes" I said to something I didn't want to do meant that I had to say "no" to something I did want to do.

Let me break it down for you with a few examples. When I said "yes" to being the PTA president, I was actually saying "no" to baking cookies with my son on Tuesday afternoons. Little Timmy's dreams of becoming the next Gordon Ramsay? Crushed. (Okay, maybe not crushed, but definitely delayed.)

When I said "yes" to taking on that extra client project over the weekend, I was saying "no" to my weekly date night with my husband. Romance? On life support. (Thank goodness my husband is more patient than I am.)

When I said "yes" to answering work emails at 10 PM, I was saying "no" to my much-needed beauty sleep. My eye bags were starting to look less like bags and more like full-on luggage. (Hello, Samsonite, is that you under my eyes?)

It was time for a change. I needed to learn the art of setting boundaries fast. And you know what? As I started setting those boundaries, something magical happened. The frustration began to melt away. The resentment? Packed its bags and took a hike. Anger? It stuck around for a bit, but eventually got the message that it wasn't welcome anymore.

I started being selective about the clients I took on. I set office hours and (gasp!) actually stuck to them. I learned to say no to projects that didn't align with my goals or values. And guess what? The world didn't end. In fact, it got a whole lot better.

Not only was I making more money, my work became more fulfilling because I was focusing on projects I truly cared about. My family remembered what I looked like without a stressed-out scowl (turns out, I'm quite pleasant when I'm not overworked - who knew?). And as a Christian? Let's just say it's a lot easier to "love thy neighbor" when you're not silently cursing them for asking for "just one more tiny favor."

Now, before you think I've got it all figured out (ha!), let me assure you - setting boundaries is an ongoing process. It's like laundry or dishes; just when you think you're done, there's more to do. But it gets easier with practice, and the payoff is worth every uncomfortable "no" you have to utter.

Reflection

When do you say yes when you want to say no? Why do you say yes?

When do you say no when you want to say yes? Why do you say no?

Is this something you want to change? If so, what's stopping you?

Bible Reading

READ MARK 1:35-39 (KJV)

Let's revisit Mark 1:35-39 and dive a little deeper. Here, we see Jesus do three things that we should replicate in our own lives. First, Jesus sets a boundary for personal time with God. Second, he makes it a practice to not immediately respond to every demand that is made of him. Third, Jesus stayed focused on His primary mission. If Jesus, with His divine nature, needed to set boundaries to achieve His goals, how important is it for us to do the same?

In what areas of your life do you find it most difficult to set boundaries? Why do you think that is?

How might setting better boundaries improve your relationship with God, yourself, and others?

In what ways can you relate to Jesus' example of setting boundaries? How does this challenge or encourage you?

Remember...

Setting boundaries isn't selfish - it's stewardship. You're taking care of the amazing person God created you to be. And when you're at your best, you're better equipped to love others and to serve God.

As we continue this journey of building healthy boundaries, keep in mind that it's a process. You might not get it perfect every time, and that's okay.

For do I now persuade men, or God? or do I seek to please men? for if I yet pleased men, I should not be the servant of Christ.
- Galatians 1:10 (KJV)

Let's dive deeper into boundaries as we tackle the sneaky beast known as people-pleasing. You know, that thing where you twist yourself into a pretzel trying to make everyone happy, only to end up feeling like a salty, dissatisfied snack yourself.

If you find yourself saying yes when you want to say no often, this section is definitely for you. People-pleasing is like trying to fill a bucket with a hole in it. No matter how much you pour in, it's never enough. Here are some practical tools to help patch that hole.

- **The Mirror Exercise:** Every morning, look in the mirror and say, "My worth is not determined by how many people I please today or who I think loves me. God loves me and that's all the love I have to have." Cheesy? *Maybe*. Effective? You bet your sweet bippy it is.

- **The Approval Audit:** Make a list of whose approval you're seeking. Then ask yourself, "Will their opinion matter in 5 years?" If not, maybe it's not worth stressing over now.

- **The People-Pleasing Pause:** Before automatically saying yes, pause and ask yourself, "Am I doing this because I want to, or because I'm afraid of disappointing someone?" Don't be so afraid of disappointing people that you sacrifice your peace. Choose based on your answer.

- **The "Good Enough" Mantra:** Remind yourself that you don't have to be perfect. "I am doing my best, and that is good enough" is a powerful phrase to combat people-pleasing tendencies.

If you're wanting to say no but having trouble finding the words, here are some practical tools to help you. First, instead of a flat no, try "Yes, I'd love to help with that bake sale. And to make that possible, I'll need to step down from the fundraising committee." This shows you're willing to contribute while maintaining balance.

Another trick is before saying yes to something, ask yourself, "Is this more important than what I'd have to give up to do it?" If the answer is no, then your answer should be no too. For persistent folks, sometimes you need to repeat your boundary calmly and without elaboration. "I'm not able to take that on" or "Do not speak to me that way" is a complete sentence. Repeat as necessary.

If you want to go the extra mile, enlist a friend or spouse to hold you accountable. Give them permission to ask you hard questions and keep you accountable to teaching people the best way to love you.

In what areas of your life do you tend to people-please the most?

How has people-pleasing affected your relationship with God?

What are some words or tricks you can use to set and hold boundaries when you feel yourself being pressured into people pleasing?

Bible Reading

READ LUKE 10:38-42 (KJV)

Martha was caught up in people-pleasing, trying to be the perfect hostess because she didn't want to be judged or thought of as someone who was lazy. Mary, on the other hand, chose to focus on what was truly important - spending time with Jesus. Jesus gently reminded Martha that it's okay to let go of the need to please everyone and instead focus on what truly matters.

Can you relate to Martha in the biblical example? How so?

What's one step you can take today to be more like Mary, focusing on what truly matters?

Today's Challenge

Today, conduct your own Approval Audit. Make a list of people whose approval you often seek. Next to each name, write why their approval is important to you. For each person, ask yourself: "Will their opinion of me matter in 5 years?" Identify one person on your list whose approval you can start caring less about. Write down one action you can take this week to reduce your need for this person's approval.

Remember, your worth comes from God, not from the approval of others. You are already approved, accepted, and loved by the One who matters most!

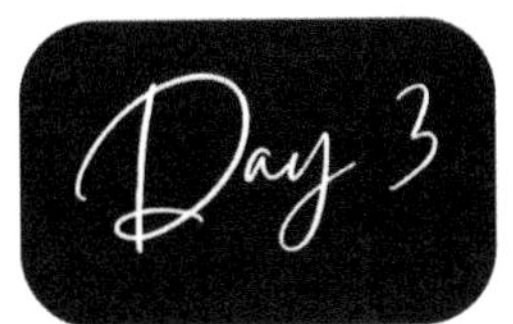

"Be not deceived: evil communications corrupt good manners." - 1 Corinthians 15:33 (KJV)

Now, let's talk about an anger trigger that is a bit heavier: *toxic relationships*. These are the relationships that leave you feeling drained, anxious, or just plain icky. They're like emotional vampires, sucking the joy right out of you.

A toxic relationship might involve constant criticism or belittling or disrespect for your boundaries. It can include emotional manipulation or a one-sided effort (you're always giving, they're always taking). Even bigger red flags are jealousy or controlling behavior as well as constant drama or conflict.

Here's the thing: forgiveness is important, absolutely. But **forgiveness doesn't mean you have to keep toxic people in your life.** You can forgive someone and still recognize that they're not a healthy presence for you.

Think of it this way: if someone had a highly contagious illness, you'd probably limit your exposure to them, right? The same goes for toxic behavior. You can wish them well from a safe distance.

So, how do you identify and address toxic relationships? Here are a few ways to start.

- **The Toxicity Test:** Write down how you feel before and after interacting with someone. If you consistently feel worse afterwards, that's a red flag.
- **The Boundary Bonanza:** Set clear, firm boundaries with toxic individuals. "I'm not comfortable discussing that" or "I need to end this conversation if you continue to speak to me that way" are good starting points.
- **The Limited Exposure Plan:** If you can't completely remove a toxic person from your life (like a family member), limit your interactions. Plan an exit strategy for gatherings, and have a support person you can call afterwards.
- **The Self-Care Surge:** After dealing with a toxic person, intentionally do something that refills your emotional tank. Whether it's prayer, a hobby, or time with positive friends, prioritize your well-being.
- **The Grace and Space Method:** Extend grace to toxic individuals - they're often acting out of their own pain. But also give yourself grace, and the space you need to heal and thrive.

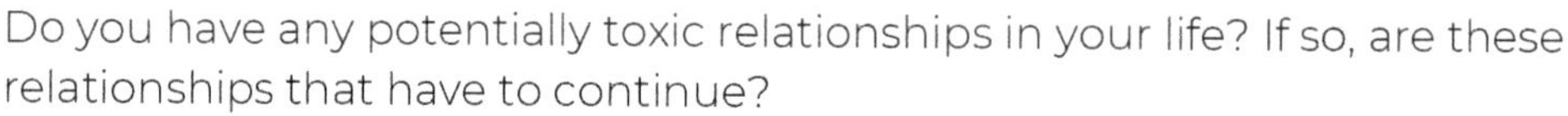

Do you have any potentially toxic relationships in your life? If so, are these relationships that have to continue?

How have these relationships affected your emotional and spiritual well-being?

Is there something that you can do to either separate yourself from this person entirely or at least limit their impact to your emotional and spiritual well-being?

What are some actions you can take today to start limiting their impact on your peace and anger?

Bible Reading

READ 1 CORINTHIANS 15:33 AND PROVERBS 22:24-25 (KJV)

The Bible warns us repeatedly about the importance of who we spend time with in this life. I've learned first hand that there are only two types of people in this world. People who lift you up and people who drag you down. While we all have our winning and losing seasons, there are those who just suck the life out of the people around them. They bring out the worst in people. If you want to live the life that God has for you, you have to avoid those people at all costs. They'll separate you from God and drag you down to their level.

What are some ways that you can improve your circle? Are there people that you need to add or remove? If so, what steps do you need to take now to do that?

Challenge

For the next week, conduct the *Toxicity Test*:

1. Identify three relationships that you suspect might be toxic.
2. Before interacting with each person, note how you feel emotionally and physically.
3. Immediately after the interaction, note your feelings again.
4. At the end of the week, review your notes. Look for patterns.
5. For relationships that consistently leave you feeling worse, brainstorm three ways you could set boundaries or limit exposure.

Remember, setting boundaries in toxic relationships isn't unchristian - it's wise stewardship of your emotional and spiritual health.

And as he lay and slept under a juniper tree, behold, then an angel touched him, and said unto him, Arise and eat. And he looked, and, behold, there was a cake baken on the coals, and a cruse of water at his head. And he did eat and drink, and laid him down again.
- 1 Kings 19:5-6 (KJV)

Let's take a little trip back in time to dive deeper with one of the Bible's greatest characters (and nap enthusiasts): our main man Elijah.

Picture this: Elijah has just had the showdown of the century with the prophets of Baal. Fire from heaven, decisive victory for Team God, the works. You'd think he'd be on top of the world, right? Maybe planning a victory lap or at least a celebratory feast?

Nope. Our boy Elijah is exhausted. He's done. Stick-a-fork-in-him finished. He's so tired that when Queen Jezebel threatens his life, instead of standing his ground, he hightails it into the wilderness and basically tells God, "I'm out. Find yourself another prophet."

Now, here's where it gets good. Does God lecture Elijah about having more faith? Does He tell him to buck up and get back to work? Nope. God looks at his worn-out prophet and essentially says, "Buddy, you need a nap and a sandwich."

I'm paraphrasing, of course, but that's the gist of 1 Kings 19:5-8. An angel comes to Elijah, gives him food and water, and tells him to rest. Not once, but twice. It's like the Biblical equivalent of your mom telling you to take a break from studying and get some sleep.

Here's the kicker: God knew exactly what Elijah needed. Just like He knows exactly what we need. Sometimes, what we need isn't a spiritual pep talk or a kick in the pants. Sometimes, what we need is rest, nourishment, and a break from the chaos.

In our go-go-go culture, it's easy to fall into the trap of thinking that running ourselves ragged is somehow noble or spiritual. But here's a truth bomb for you: exhaustion is not a fruit of the Spirit. You won't find "burnout" listed alongside love, joy, and peace in Galatians.

God cares about our physical and emotional well-being just as much as our spiritual health. In fact, they're all connected. It's hard to love others when you're running on fumes. It's tough to experience joy when you're stressed to the max. And peace? Forget about it if you're constantly overcommitting yourself.

How often do you prioritize self-care in your life and what do you do?

What are some signs that you might be neglecting self-care?

How might regular self-care improve your relationship with God and others?

What are 3 things you can do this week to take better care of yourself?

Bible Reading

READ 1 KINGS 19:5-8 AND LUKE 5:16 (KJV)

We know that Elijah was blessed when God saw and met his physical needs. Yet even Jesus, who had the most important mission in the history of the world, took time for self-care. Jesus, despite the constant demands on His time and energy, made it a priority to retreat, rest, and reconnect with the Father. If the Son of God needed this, how much more do we?

In what ways can you relate to Elijah's burnout?

How does God's response to Elijah encourage you?

Today's Challenge

For the next week, identify one small act of self-care you can do each day. It could be a 10-minute walk, reading a chapter of a book you enjoy, or simply sitting in silence for a few minutes. Schedule this self-care activity into your day, just like you would any other important appointment. Before each self-care activity, note your stress level on a scale of 1-10. After the activity, note your stress level again. At the end of the week, reflect on how these small acts of self-care affected your overall well-being and your ability to handle stress. Remember, taking care of yourself isn't selfish - it's necessary. You can't pour from an empty cup, and you can't serve God and others effectively if you're running on empty.

What To Do Now

Make sure to log in and gain access to additional reflection questions, closing prayers, group activities, and additional resources at www.youarenotcalled.com.

As we move forward, we'll be exploring how to maintain these boundaries and self-care practices in the face of life's inevitable challenges. In the next chapter, we'll dive into:

- Strategies for reinforcing boundaries when they're challenged
- How to communicate your boundaries effectively to others
- Dealing with guilt when setting boundaries
- Balancing flexibility and firmness in your boundaries
- How boundaries can actually improve your relationships

Remember, setting boundaries and practicing self-care aren't selfish - they're essential for your well-being and your ability to love and serve others effectively.

Make sure to login to your account at youarenotcalled.com to get this weeks resources!

Weekly Recap

- **Day 1: The Importance of Boundaries**
  - We learned that every "yes" is actually a "no" to something else.
  - We saw how Jesus set boundaries in His ministry.
  - We practiced the "Sleep On It" Technique for better decision-making.
- **Day 2: Combating People-Pleasing**
  - We explored strategies to overcome the need for others' approval.
  - We learned from Martha and Mary about choosing what truly matters.
  - We conducted an Approval Audit to identify whose opinions we overvalue.
- **Day 3: Recognizing and Handling Toxic Relationships**
  - We identified characteristics of toxic relationships.
  - We learned from David's handling of his relationship with Saul.
  - We practiced the Toxicity Test to evaluate our relationships.
- **Day 4: The Power of Self-Care**
  - We saw how God prioritized Elijah's physical needs during his burnout.
  - We learned from Jesus' example of withdrawing for prayer and rest.
  - We committed to a daily Self-Care Surge.

Week Eight

Praise ye the LORD. Blessed is the man that feareth the LORD, that delighteth greatly in his commandments. His seed shall be mighty upon earth: the generation of the upright shall be blessed.
- Psalm 112:1-2 (KJV)

Alright, you've made it this far, and I'm impressed! We're about to dive into some next-level anger management territory. Think of it as the graduate course in keeping your cool. Or, if you prefer, the black belt class in emotional kung fu. So strap in, because things are about to get real (but also hopefully a little funny, because let's face it, laughter is the best medicine... except for actual medicine, of course).

Let's start with a fun fact: Did you know that anger can be passed down through families faster than your great-aunt Edna's questionable fruitcake recipe? It's true! Generational patterns of anger are like the world's worst family heirloom. "Here, darling, have this priceless vase and my hair-trigger temper. Enjoy!"

But here's the good news: unlike that vase (which, let's be honest, is ugly and you'd love an excuse to "accidentally" break it), you don't have to keep this inheritance. You can be the one to break the chain.

First, let's talk about recognizing these inherited anger patterns. Maybe you've noticed that you react to stress the same way your dad does. Or perhaps you've caught yourself using the exact same angry phrases your mom used when you were a kid. If you've ever thought, "Oh no, I've become my parents!" while in the middle of an angry outburst, congratulations! You've just spotted a generational pattern.

Now, before you start blaming Great-Great-Grandpa Joe for your anger issues, let's look at what the Bible has to say about this. In Exodus 20:5-6, God talks about the sins of the fathers being visited upon the children to the third and fourth generation. Sounds pretty grim, right? But keep reading! He goes on to say that He shows love to a thousand generations of those who love Him and keep His commandments.

In other words, yes, negative patterns can be passed down, but God's love and the potential for change are so much stronger and far-reaching. It's like having a tiny pebble of family dysfunction and a whole mountain of God's grace. I don't know about you, but I'm putting my money on the mountain!

So, how do we break this cycle? You'll find practical steps to break these bonds on the next page.

Remember, you have the power to change your family tree. Your future kids or grandkids might just thank you for not passing down the family "anger heirloom." Instead, you can pass down peace, patience, and maybe a less questionable recipe than Aunt Edna's fruitcake.

Breaking The Generational Curse Of Anger

This road that you're walking isn't easy. I'm so proud of you for deciding to be different. Below, you'll find a few ways to make breaking the anger habit a little bit easier.

1 **Acknowledge the pattern.** You can't fix what you don't admit exists. It's like trying to cure a disease without diagnosing it first. You'll just end up taking a lot of unnecessary cough syrup.

2 **Forgive your ancestors.** I know, easier said than done. But remember, hurt people hurt people. Your sister, brother, aunt, uncle, parents or grandparents were likely dealing with their own unresolved issues. Forgiveness doesn't mean what they did was okay; it means you're releasing yourself from the burden of bitterness.

3 **Choose a different response.** When you feel that familiar anger rising, pause. Take a deep breath. Ask yourself, "Is this my authentic reaction, or am I just playing out a script I've inherited?" Then, consciously choose a different response.

4 **Seek God's healing.** Pray for God to heal those generational wounds and to help you establish new, healthier patterns. It's like asking for a holy software update for your emotional operating system. Be patient with yourself.

Breaking generational patterns is not an overnight process. It's more like trying to redirect a river – it takes time, effort, and probably a few soggy socks along the way.

Bible Reading

READ 2 KINGS 22 (KJV)

King Josiah, as recorded in 2 Kings 22-23, broke a cycle of idolatry and disobedience that had lasted for generations. Despite being raised in a corrupt environment, Josiah chose to seek God and bring reform to Judah. He didn't let his family's past dictate his future. Talk about a generational pattern breaker!

What does Josiah do when he realizes he has been doing the wrong thing?

Is there anything that you have been doing that you thought was right or normal that you now realize is wrong? If so, what steps have you taken or can you take to make it right?

Challenge

Reflect on your family's anger patterns. Write down phrases, reactions, or triggers that run in your family. Be honest with yourself – this isn't about blame, it's about awareness.

Remember...

Remember, you have the power to change your family tree and the fruit that comes from it. Your future kids or grandkids will thank you for not passing down the family "anger heirloom." Instead, you can pass down peace, joy, and patience.

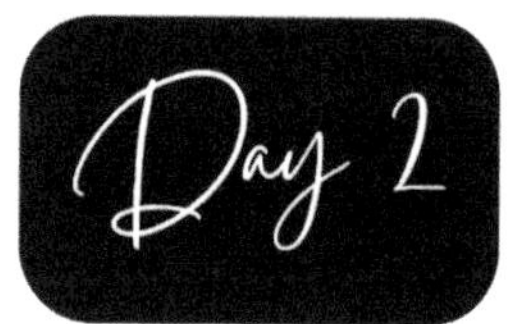

"Be not overcome of evil, but overcome evil with good."
- Romans 12:21 (KJV)

Alright, folks, grab your metaphorical referee whistles because we're about to dive into the high-stakes world of family dynamics. It's time to talk about the not-so-fun game of "Who Can Blow Their Top First?" that often plays out in our homes.

Meet the Johnson family: Mike, Sarah, and their two kids, Emma (age 10) and Liam (age 7). On paper, they're the picture-perfect family. In reality? They're more like a powder keg with a very short fuse.

Mike's stressed about work and snaps at Sarah for the tiniest things. Sarah, feeling unappreciated, takes it out on the kids. Emma slams doors and gives the silent treatment, while Liam throws epic tantrums that would put a Hollywood diva to shame.

One day, after a particularly explosive family dinner (where more harsh words were thrown than actual food was eaten), they all retreat to separate corners of the house, licking their emotional wounds.

But here's where it gets interesting. Sarah, in a moment of quiet desperation, whispers a prayer: "God, we can't go on like this. Please help us."

And you know what? God answers. Not with a bolt of lightning or a booming voice from the heavens, but with a gentle nudge towards change.

Sarah calls a family meeting. Instead of pointing fingers, she starts with an apology. "I'm sorry for letting my frustration out on you guys. I love you all, and I want us to do better." Mike, taken aback, follows suit. The kids, seeing their parents own up to their mistakes, slowly open up too. Together, they decide to implement some new family rules:

- The "Pause Button": When anyone feels anger rising, they can call "Pause!" and take a 5-minute breather.

- The "I Feel" Rule: Express feelings without blame. "I feel hurt when..." instead of "You always..."

- The "Appreciation Station": Each day, everyone shares one thing they appreciate about each family member.

It's not an overnight fix. There are still heated moments and missteps. But slowly, the atmosphere in the Johnson home begins to change. They're learning to navigate their anger together, as a team, rather than using it as a weapon against each other.
Sound like a fairytale? Maybe... But who said you couldn't live in a fairytale?

I mean don't most of us go into marriage and building a family with a Disney-esque type view on what it will be like on to find that it is in fact a beautiful institution where you promise to love someone forever, and then five minutes later, you're contemplating how to smother them with a pillow because they're chewing too loudly? (Just kidding! Please don't smother your spouse. It's generally frowned upon in most social circles.)

If you're not married yet, amazing! The things that we're about to discuss are going to save you some serious heart ache if you can learn and master these principles now...before you really need them.

The thing about marriage is that it's intimate. And with intimacy comes vulnerability, which means your spouse has a front-row seat to all your emotional highs and lows. They're also often the safest target for your anger because you know they're not going anywhere (well, hopefully not). So how do we handle anger in marriage? Here are some tips:

- **Remember you're on the same team.** It's not you vs. your spouse; it's both of you vs. the problem. Unless the problem is their sock-leaving habit, in which case it's definitely them. (I'm kidding... mostly.)

- **Use "I" statements.** Instead of "You always leave your socks on the floor!", try "I feel frustrated when I see socks on the floor." It's less accusatory and more likely to lead to a productive conversation.

- **Take a time-out.** Sometimes, you need to step away and cool off before you say something you'll regret. It's like putting yourself in the naughty corner, but for adults.

- **Pray together.** There's something powerful about bringing your frustrations to God as a couple. Plus, it's hard to stay mad at someone when you're holding hands and praying.

Okay that's great that my husband and I can deal with each other but what about dealing with the children, you ask? Ah, children. Those precious gifts from God who have the uncanny ability to push every single one of your buttons, often all at once. One minute, you're looking at them thinking, "I would die for you," and the next minute, you're wondering, "Is it too late to return them?"

Managing anger as a parent is crucial because little eyes are always watching. Remember that their behavior often isn't personal. Your toddler isn't having a meltdown in the grocery store just to embarrass you (even if it feels that way). Also, take care of yourself. A well-rested, well-fed parent is much less likely to lose their cool. You can't pour from an empty cup, and you can't parent well from an empty emotional tank.

Even more importantly, model good anger management. Show them how to handle frustration in a healthy way. They're more likely to do what you do than what you say. Ask for forgiveness when you mess up. Because you will mess up. We all do. Showing your kids that even parents make mistakes and need forgiveness is a valuable lesson.

How might your expressions of anger be affecting your spouse and children?

Can you identify any patterns of anger in your family that might be cyclical (i.e., one person's anger triggering another's)?

What are some ways you can create a more positive emotional environment in your home?

How can you apply the principle of anger management in your daily interactions with your kids?

Bible Reading

READ COLOSSIANS 3:21 (KJV)

Paul, in his letter to the Colossians, drops some serious parenting wisdom. He warns against embittering children. This isn't just about avoiding angry outbursts. It's about creating an environment where our kids feel secure, valued, and encouraged. It's about modeling the kind of emotional regulation we want to see in our children. Game changer: our spouses need the same thing.

Today's Challenge

For the next week, let's give your family dynamics an emotion makeover. Implement the Johnson family's three rules: The Pause Button, The "I Feel" Rule, and The Appreciation Station. Each evening, have a family check-in. Ask each member: What made you happy today? What frustrated you today? How did you handle your frustrations?

Practice active listening when your spouse or children express their feelings. Repeat back what you heard to ensure understanding. Before reacting in anger to your spouse or kids, ask yourself: "Will this response encourage or discourage them?" At the end of the week, have a family meeting to discuss what worked, what didn't, and what you want to continue doing.

Remember: creating a peaceful home isn't about being perfect. It's about progress, grace, and a whole lot of love. Your family is a team, and God is your ultimate coach. He's not looking for flawless performance, but for hearts that are willing to grow and change.

You might have some fumbles along the way, and that's okay. The important thing is that you keep getting back up, dusting yourselves off, and trying again. With God's help, you can turn your home from a battleground into a training ground for love, joy, peace, patience, kindness, goodness, faithfulness, gentleness, and self-control.

And whatsoever ye do, do it heartily, as to the Lord, and not unto men.
- Colossians 3:23 (KJV)

We're about to dive into the wild world of workplace woes and scholarly struggles. You know, those situations where your boss or teacher seems to have the decision-making skills of a magic 8-ball and the communication clarity of a broken radio.

Meet Sarah, a dedicated marketing executive who's pretty sure her boss, Dave, got his management degree from a cereal box. Dave has a special talent for scheduling meetings that could have been emails, creating "urgent" projects at 4:55 PM on a Friday, and taking credit for Sarah's ideas.

Then there's Tom, a high school junior whose history teacher, Mrs. Johnson, seems to think "group project" means "let the overachievers do all the work while the rest play Candy Crush." She has a knack for assigning essays on obscure topics that even Google struggles to find information about.

One particularly trying day, Sarah finds herself in a meeting where Dave is proudly presenting her project as his own brilliant idea. She can feel her blood pressure rising faster than Dave's inflated ego. Meanwhile, across town, Tom is staring at a group project assignment sheet, realizing he's been paired with the class clown and the kid who thinks the Civil War was fought by Captain America and Iron Man.

Both Sarah and Tom are at their wit's end, ready to explode like a shaken soda can. But just as they're about to unleash a tirade that would make a sailor blush, they remember a little nugget of wisdom from Colossians 3:23.

Instead of blowing up, Sarah takes a deep breath and reminds herself that ultimately, she's working for God, not Dave. She decides to continue giving her best, not for Dave's approval, but as an act of worship to God.

Tom, fighting the urge to bang his head against his history book, chooses to see this as an opportunity to practice patience and leadership. He decides to approach the project with enthusiasm, viewing it as a chance to help his classmates engage with history in a meaningful way.

Now, did this suddenly make Dave less of a credit-stealing cappuccino-brain or transform Mrs. Johnson into a pinnacle of educational excellence? Nope. But it did change Sarah and Tom's perspectives and responses.

Sarah continued to produce excellent work, and eventually, her consistency and quality caught the attention of upper management, leading to a well-deserved promotion (bye-bye, Dave!). Tom's positive attitude not only helped his group ace the project but also earned him the respect of his classmates and teacher.

Bible Reading READ COLOSSIANS 3:23-24 (KJV)

Paul drops this truth bomb on us: our work, whether in the office, classroom, or anywhere else, is ultimately for God. This perspective shift is like putting on spiritual bifocals - suddenly, we can see beyond the immediate frustrations to the greater purpose of our efforts.

This doesn't mean we become doormats or ignore workplace injustices. Rather, it means we approach our work with integrity, excellence, and a positive attitude, regardless of who's in charge or how they're acting.

How might your work or studies change if you consciously approached them as working for God rather than human authorities?

What are some practical ways you can remind yourself of this perspective when facing frustrating situations at work or school?

How can viewing your work as service to God help manage anger towards incompetent or unfair leadership?

Challenge

For the next week, let's put Colossians 3:23 into practice:

Each morning, before starting work or school, remind yourself: "Today, I'm working for God, not for human masters." When you encounter a frustrating situation with a boss, teacher, or coworker, pause and ask yourself: "How would I handle this if Jesus was my direct supervisor?" At the end of each day, reflect on one way you demonstrated excellence in your work or studies, not for human praise, but as an offering to God.

Keep In Mind...

Remember, you're not just pushing papers, crunching numbers, or cramming for exams. You're building character, shaping your testimony, and worshiping God through your work. Your incompetent boss or clueless teacher? They're supporting actors in the grand production of your spiritual growth.

So the next time Dave takes credit for your idea or Mrs. Johnson assigns another group project from hell, take a deep breath, shoot up a quick prayer, and remember - you've got the best Boss in the universe, and He sees every stapler you don't throw, every eye you don't roll, and every positive attitude you choose in spite of it all.

Now go out there and work it, honey - not for that corner office or perfect GPA (though those would be nice), but for the standing ovation you'll get from the King of Kings. Talk about the ultimate performance review!

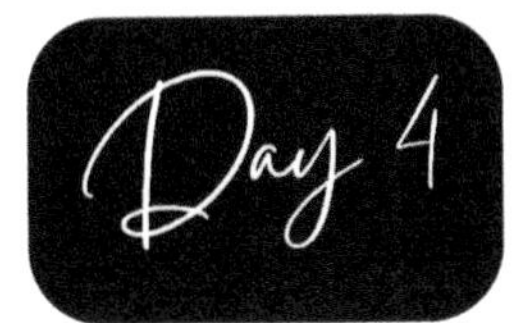

The LORD is nigh unto them that are of a broken heart;
And saveth such as be of a contrite spirit.
- Psalm 34:18 (KJV)

Let's talk about something that often gatecrashes our emotional shindig uninvited: grief. It's like that party guest who shows up in a Halloween costume when it's not a costume party. Except instead of just being awkward, grief often comes disguised as anger, ready to flip tables and pick fights with anyone in sight.

Picture this: Sarah, a usually cheerful soccer mom, finds herself snapping at her kids over the tiniest things. Her road rage has reached epic proportions, and don't even get her started on the incompetent barista who can't seem to get her coffee order right. To the outside world, Sarah looks like she's auditioning for the role of "Angriest Woman in Suburbia."

But here's the twist – Sarah isn't just angry. She's grieving. Six months ago, she lost her mom to cancer, and she hasn't allowed herself to fully process that loss. Instead, her grief has put on an anger costume and is wreaking havoc on her life.

One day, after yelling at her daughter for spilling milk (literally crying over spilled milk – oh, the irony), Sarah catches a glimpse of herself in the mirror. She barely recognizes the red-faced, wild-eyed woman staring back at her. At that moment, she realizes something needs to change.

Sarah starts seeing a therapist, who helps her understand that her anger is actually grief in disguise. She learns that it's okay to be sad, to miss her mom, to feel the full weight of her loss. As she allows herself to grieve properly, guess what happens? The anger begins to subside.

Now, I'm not saying Sarah turns into a zen master overnight. There are still tough days, moments when grief sucker-punches her out of nowhere. But now, instead of letting it masquerade as anger, she recognizes it for what it is. She allows herself to feel it, to honor her mom's memory, and then to keep moving forward.

Can you identify any anger in your life that might actually be unprocessed grief? What losses might you need to acknowledge?

In what ways might allowing yourself to grieve properly help reduce anger in your life?

How can you create space in your life to process grief in a healthy way?

Bible Reading

READ PSALM 34:18 (KJV)

David, the man after God's own heart, was no stranger to grief. In 2 Samuel, we see him pleading with God for the life of his sick child. For seven days, he fasts and prays. But when the child dies, David's response is surprising. He gets up, washes, and worships God. He acknowledges his grief but doesn't let it control him.

In Psalm 34, likely written during one of his many trials, David reminds us that God is close to the brokenhearted. He doesn't tell us to buck up or get over it. Instead, he assures us that in our deepest pain, God is right there with us.

Today's Challenge

Take 5 minutes to sit quietly and ask yourself, "What losses am I carrying that I haven't fully acknowledged?" If you identify any, write them down. It could be big losses like a death, or smaller ones like the loss of a dream or expectation. For each loss, allow yourself to feel the sadness. You might cry, you might not – both are okay. Say a simple prayer, something like, "God, I'm hurting over [this loss]. Thank you for being close to me in my pain."

Remember, grief isn't something to be conquered or beaten. It's a journey, and it's okay to take that journey at your own pace. The goal isn't to "get over it," but to move through it, allowing God to walk with you every step of the way.

You're not weak for grieving – you're human. And in your humanity, you're deeply loved by a God who knows what it is to weep. So let those tears flow when they need to. Your Heavenly Father is right there, ready with the spiritual equivalent of a warm hug and a box of tissues.

What's Next...

Remember, managing anger isn't about never feeling angry. It's about handling that anger in a way that honors God, respects others, and doesn't leave you feeling like you need to apologize to everyone you've ever met. It's a journey, not a destination, and it's okay if you're not perfect at it right away (or ever, because, you know, we're human).

As you move forward, consider which of these areas you need to focus on most. Is it breaking generational patterns? Improving family dynamics? Changing your perspective at work? Or perhaps processing hidden grief? Whatever it is, know that with God's help and the tools you've learned, you're well-equipped to face these challenges. Keep growing, keep learning, and keep letting God's love transform your anger into something beautiful.

As we close this chapter on managing anger in complex situations, we look forward to next week where we'll explore how to continue growing long after we've completed this book. Make sure to login to your account at youarenotcalled.com to get this weeks resources!

Weekly Recap

- **Day 1: Breaking Generational Patterns of Anger**
    - We learned that anger can be inherited like a family heirloom.
    - We discovered practical steps to break generational anger cycles.
    - Key takeaway: With God's help, we can rewrite our family's emotional legacy.
- **Day 2: Anger in Marriage and Family**
    - We explored the Johnson family's journey from chaos to harmony.
    - We learned strategies for managing anger in marriage and parenting.
    - Key takeaway: Creating a peaceful home is about progress, grace, and love.
- **Day 3: Anger at Work and School**
    - We met Sarah and Tom, dealing with frustrating work and school situations.
    - We learned to approach work as serving God, not human masters (Colossians 3:23).
    - Key takeaway: Our work is an act of worship, regardless of human leadership.
- **Day 4: Grief and Anger**
    - We explored how grief often masquerades as anger.
    - We studied David's example of healthy grieving in Psalm 34:18.
    - Key takeaway: Acknowledging and processing grief can help manage anger.

Week Nine

"The LORD is nigh unto them that are of a broken heart; and saveth such as be of a contrite spirit."
- Philippians 1:6 (KJV)

We've made it to the home stretch! Before we dive in, I want to share a little secret with you. Now, I'd love to tell you that after writing this book, I've achieved enlightenment, my halo is polished to a high shine, and I float serenely through life without a hint of anger. But let's be real - that's about as likely as me winning an Olympic gold medal in synchronized swimming (trust me, you don't want to see that).

The truth is, just like you, I'm still on this journey. It's an ongoing dance between battling anger and my emotions, setting boundaries, taking care of myself, getting out of alignment, and course-correcting. Some days I'm gracefully gliding across the dance floor of life, and other days I'm stepping on toes and tripping over my own feet.

But you know what? That's okay. Because just like you, I am learning and growing with Jesus every day. And that, my friends, is why we need to practice.

When it comes to growing in Christ, the Bible has plenty to say. It's like God knew we'd need some encouragement in this department (spoiler alert: He did). Let's check out a few key verses.

> Philippians 1:6, tells us, "Being confident of this, that he who began a good work in you will carry it on to completion until the day of Christ Jesus."

It's like God is saying, "Don't worry, I've got this project under control, and I'm not about to abandon it halfway through!" So the next time you feel like you're not making progress, remember - God's not done with you yet!

> Colossians 1:10 encourages us to "walk in a manner worthy of the Lord, fully pleasing to him: bearing fruit in every good work and increasing in the knowledge of God."

This isn't about perfection. It's about progress. It's like God is cheering us on saying, "That's it! One step at a time! You're getting there!"

In what areas of your life have you seen progress in managing anger? Where do you still struggle?

How can you "let your roots grow down into Him" in your daily life?

Challenge For The Week

Set aside 5 minutes each morning this week. Begin with a simple prayer: "God, I ask for Your wisdom today. Help me see situations through Your eyes and respond with Your love." Keep a small journal or use a notes app on your phone. Throughout the day, jot down any insights or "aha" moments you have.

Remember, wisdom isn't just about knowing things; it's about applying God's truth to our daily lives. It's practical, it's powerful, and best of all - we can ask for it!

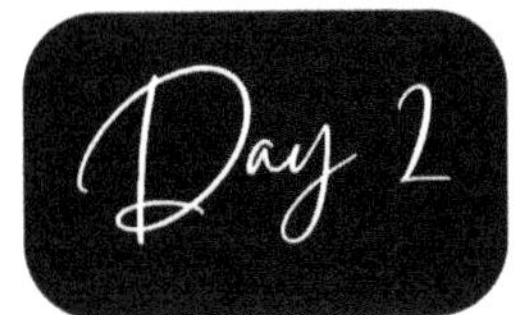

If any of you lack wisdom, let him ask of God, that giveth to all men liberally, and upbraideth not; and it shall be given him.
- James 1:5 (KJV)

Throughout this journey, we've covered more ground than a hyperactive toddler in a toy store. We've talked about:

- Recognizing anger and its impact on our lives
- Understanding the power of choice in our reactions
- The importance of forgiveness (even when it's tough)
- How love can transform our relationships and attitudes
- Setting healthy boundaries to prevent resentment
- Taking care of ourselves (because you can't pour from an empty cup)

And here's the kicker: the only thing holding you back from overcoming your anger is... drumroll please... **YOU**!

There's an African proverb that says, "*If there is no enemy within, the enemy outside can do no harm.*" When we get our inner world in order, the outer world becomes much easier to handle. It's like tidying up your spiritual and emotional house - suddenly, those external annoyances don't seem so overwhelming.

Now, here's where the rubber meets the road, where the cookie meets the milk, where the... okay, I'll stop with the analogies. The point is, all of this knowledge is great, but it's useless if we don't put it into practice. We need to make the choice every single day to apply what we've learned.

It's about choosing grace when someone cuts us off in traffic (even if our first instinct is to unleash a string of words that would make a sailor blush).

It's about choosing gratitude when we're stuck in a long line at the grocery store (instead of mentally cataloging all the ways we could redesign the store for maximum efficiency).

It's about choosing not to board that emotional train when our buttons get pushed (even if that train looks mighty tempting and is headed to Righteous Indignation Station).

Can you identify a recent situation where your own thoughts or actions sabotaged your efforts to manage anger? What internal dialogue or beliefs contributed to this self-sabotage?

The African proverb suggests that our internal state greatly influences our external experiences. In what ways might your inner critic be amplifying the anger-inducing situations in your life?

Imagine yourself as your own best ally in managing anger. What specific encouragement, advice, or support would you offer to yourself? How can you start implementing this self-support in your daily life?

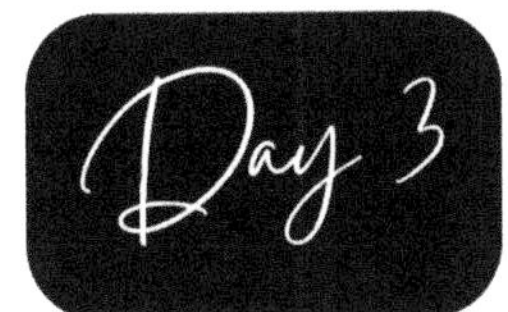

" For we are his workmanship, created in Christ Jesus unto good works, which God hath before ordained that we should walk in them."
- Ephesians 2:10 (KJV)

You know how in every great superhero movie, there's that pivotal moment when our hero discovers their true identity? Well, consider this your pivotal moment. Jesus didn't just give you a fancy cape and a cool catchphrase. Oh no, in our Bible reading for today in Matthew 5, He went all out and called you "the salt of the earth" and "the light of the world." Now, before you start sprinkling yourself on french fries or trying to screw yourself into a lamp socket, let's break down what He really meant.

When Jesus says you're salt, He's not just throwing out condiment metaphors for kicks. Salt preserves, flavors, and purifies. In other words, you're here to keep the good stuff from going bad, add some heavenly zest to this bland world, and clean up the mess sin leaves behind. And light? Well, you're not just here to illuminate – you're here to guide, inspire, and drive away the darkness. You're basically a walking, talking lighthouse, my friend!

Now, here's where it gets really good. You know that fruit of the Spirit stuff – love, joy, peace, and all that jazz? It's not just a wish list or a set of New Year's resolutions you'll never keep. Nope, it's your spiritual DNA, your birthright as a child of God. These qualities are already within you, part of your new nature in Christ. Your job isn't to attain them; it's to let them flourish.

Let's break it down with a real-life example...

Meet Rebecca. Rebecca had a choice to make. She'd just found out that she'd been passed over for a promotion at work, and the position had been given to her coworker, Jessie. Rebecca had two options:

- Option 1: Give in to anger and resentment. She could stew in her frustration, bad-mouth her co-worker to others, and let her bitterness affect her work performance.

- Option 2: Choose joy and peace. She could congratulate Jessie, reflect on areas where she could improve, and trust that God had a plan for her career path.

Rebecca chose Option 2. Was it easy? Nope. Did she have moments where she wanted to scream into her pillow? You bet. But by choosing joy and peace, she maintained her integrity, kept her work relationships intact, and opened herself up to new opportunities. A few months later, an even better position opened up in another department, and her positive attitude and strong work ethic made her the perfect candidate.

The choice is always yours, and so are the results of that choice.

Now, here's something crucial to understand. Releasing yourself from the bondage of anger isn't just about making your life easier (although that's a pretty sweet perk). It does three crucial things:

- **It unlocks what Jesus died to give you.** Anger separates you from God. It's like spiritual static, disrupting your connection with the divine. It distracts you, disables you, and steals your joy, peace, and ability to love. By letting go of anger, you're clearing the airwaves, allowing God's love and grace to flow freely into your life.

- **It makes you a powerful warrior for the Kingdom of God.** You are called to be a mighty warrior for Christ. If you allow anger to distract and delay you, you'll not be able to achieve what you could for the Kingdom. It's like trying to run a race with your shoelaces tied together - you might make some progress, but you're not going to reach your full potential.

- **It allows you to be a loving example of Christ.** You may be the only Jesus that someone sees which makes you a pretty powerful instrument for the Kingdom of God.

Remember, you have to let go of who you are not to become who you are meant to be in Christ. It's like trying to fill a cup that's already full - you've got to empty out the old to make room for the new.

Bible Reading

READ MATTHEW 5:13-14 (KJV)

Salt was incredibly valuable in ancient times, used for preserving food, enhancing flavor, and even as a form of currency. Light, of course, dispels darkness and allows people to see clearly. By calling us salt and light, Jesus is emphasizing our potential to positively influence the world around us. Remember, you're called to be salt not salty.

How might your daily life look different if you fully embraced your identity as "salt and light" in the world?

What does it mean to you personally to be "light" in a world that often seems dark?

How might fully embracing this identity as salt and light help you overcome anger and negativity in your life?

Keep In Mind...

Remember, you are God's masterpiece, created for a purpose. By affirming your true identity and living it out, you're not just changing yourself – you're changing the world around you!

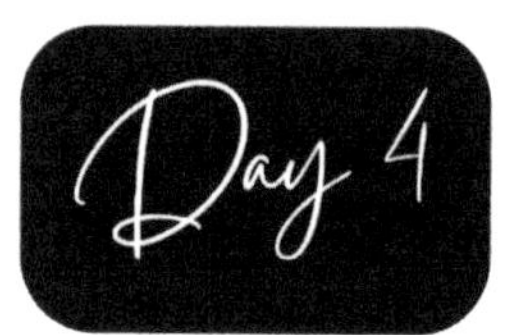

"Rooted and built up in him, and stablished in the faith, as ye have been taught, abounding therein with thanksgiving." - Colossians 2:7 (KJV)

Can we have a heart-to-heart for a moment? I know we've been on quite a journey together through this book, tackling some pretty hefty topics like anger, forgiveness, and boundaries. We've laughed, we've probably cried (or at least felt a strong urge to throw the book across the room a time or two), and hopefully, we've grown.

Now, as we come to the end of this adventure, I want to tell you something important.

I may not know many things for sure in this crazy world of ours. I can't tell you why socks mysteriously disappear in the laundry or why autocorrect seems to have a vendetta against coherent communication. But there are a few things I know with absolute certainty, and here they are:

- **You are loved.** Not just in a casual "Oh, that's nice" kind of way, but in a deep, unconditional, move-heaven-and-earth kind of way. The Creator of the universe looks at you and says, "That one. That's my masterpiece."

- **You are worthy.** Your worth isn't determined by your accomplishments, your mistakes, or what others think of you. It's inherent, given to you by God Himself. You're worthy simply because you exist.

- **You are capable.** You have strengths and abilities that are uniquely yours. God has equipped you for every good work He has planned for you.

- **You are above only and not beneath.** You're not meant to live a life of defeat or mediocrity. You're called to rise above, to live victoriously.

- **You are not alone.** Even in your darkest moments, when it feels like the whole world has turned its back on you, God is right there with you. He's never left and He never will.

- **Your story is still being written.** No matter what chapter you're in right now - even if it feels like a really lousy chapter - it's not the end. God's still writing, and He's really good at plot twists and redemption arcs.

As we finish this ride together, let's take a moment to celebrate you and the masterpiece of who you are and who you are becoming on this crazy journey that we call life.

You've stuck with this journey, you've learned new concepts, and you've been practicing new skills. That's huge and I am so proud of you!

Remember, progress, not perfection, is the goal. You're growing, you're learning, and you're becoming more like Christ every day. And that, my friend, is worth celebrating.

Looking back on your journey through this book, what small changes or improvements in managing your anger can you identify? How have these "small things" contributed to your overall growth?

Can you recall a recent situation where you responded to anger differently than you would have before starting this journey? How does acknowledging this progress make you feel?

In what ways have you seen God's hand in your "small wins" throughout this process? How might celebrating these victories fuel your motivation to continue growing?

Remember that this is really just the beginning of your journey. You're now armed with more tools than a superhero's utility belt to tackle anger and live a life full of love, wisdom, and really good boundaries.

Will you still get angry sometimes? Probably. Will you still have days where you want to flip a table or two? Most likely. (Just make sure it's not an expensive table, okay?) But now you have the knowledge and the practices to handle those moments with grace, wisdom, and maybe even a touch of humor.

So go forth and practice! Choose love over anger, grace over grudges, and wisdom over knee-jerk reactions. And on the days when you mess up (because we all do), remember that God's not done with you yet. He's still working, still molding, still transforming you into the amazing person He created you to be.

May your boundaries be strong, your love be abundant, and may you always remember that you are fearfully and wonderfully made - occasional angry outbursts and all. Now go out there and show the world what love looks like!

- **Day 1: The Journey of Growth**
  - We acknowledged that growth in Christ is an ongoing process.
  - We learned that God is continually working in us (Philippians 1:6).
  - We started the practice of daily asking God for wisdom.
- **Day 2: Putting Knowledge into Practice**
  - We reviewed key concepts from our journey.
  - We emphasized the importance of daily choices in applying what we've learned.
  - We explored practical ways to choose grace, gratitude, and emotional control.
- **Day 3: Your True Identity in Christ**
  - We discovered our identity as "salt and light" in the world (Matthew 5).
  - We learned that the fruit of the Spirit is our spiritual DNA.
  - We saw how embracing our true identity can help us overcome anger.
- **Day 4: Reflection and Moving Forward**
  - We received affirmations of our worth and capability in Christ.
  - We began the practice of celebrating our progress.

Dear Heavenly Father,

We come before You with hearts full of gratitude for the journey You've led us on through this study. Thank You for Your patience, Your grace, and Your ongoing work in our lives.

Lord, we acknowledge that we're still growing, still learning, and still in need of Your guidance every day. Help us to continue applying the principles we've learned, to choose love over anger, grace over grudges, and wisdom over knee-jerk reactions.

Father, we ask for Your continued wisdom as we navigate life's challenges. Help us to set healthy boundaries, to practice self-care, and to extend forgiveness even when it's difficult. Remind us daily of Your unfailing love and the freedom we have in Christ.

We pray for strength to put into practice what we've learned, for courage to face our struggles, and for humility to celebrate even small victories. May our lives be a testament to Your transforming power.

Thank You for the support of this group and the encouragement we've found in each other. As we go forward, help us to be beacons of Your peace and love in a world that so desperately needs it.

In Jesus' name, we pray. Amen.

Celebration Time!

At the end of each week for the next month, write down three ways you've grown or made progress, no matter how small. These can be related to anger management, spiritual growth, or any area of your life. Share these wins with a trusted friend or family member while you both celebrate over a little treat!

Remember, as our scripture focus says, when we build our lives on Christ, our faith grows strong and we overflow with thankfulness. Celebrating our progress is a way of recognizing and thanking God for His ongoing work in our lives.

Sweet Sister,

You've just completed something truly significant. Those pages you turned? Each one represented a step toward freedom. Those exercises you completed? Each one was an act of courage. The prayers you prayed? Each one was heard by a God who loves you deeply.

I see you. I see the work you've put in. I see your heart's desire for lasting change. And can I share something I've learned in my own journey? The most powerful moments of transformation often happen after closing the last page of a book – but only if we have the right support system in place.

How many times have you finished a book, felt inspired to change, but found yourself slipping back into old patterns a few weeks later? Those moments when anger tries to creep back in... when old triggers resurface... when you need someone who gets it to remind you of how far you've come...
That's exactly why The Sisterhood exists.

Picture yourself three months from now:

- Sharing your victories (big and small) with sisters who genuinely celebrate with you
- Having a safe space to be completely honest about your struggles
- Blessed with friendships that go far beyond small talk
- Growing deeper in your faith alongside women who share your values
- Finding practical solutions for daily challenges from sisters who've been there

The Sisterhood isn't just another Facebook group or casual gathering. It's your spiritual village – a place where the principles you've learned become living, breathing practices. It's where "I'll pray for you" turns into immediate, powerful prayer. Where "you've got this" comes from women who truly understand your journey.

Here's the thing: The enemy wants you to believe that reading this book was enough – that you can handle the rest on your own. But God's design is so much better. He's gathering His daughters together, creating bonds that the world can't understand and breakthrough that only comes in community.

The best part? You can join us today. Simply visit www.missiondrivensisters.com to meet your new spiritual family. You've laid the foundation through this book. Now, let's build something beautiful together. Your sisters are waiting with open arms.

With joy and expectation,

Bridget

P.S. A year from now, you'll wish you had started today. Take that next step toward lasting freedom at www.missiondrivensisters.com. Your seat at the table is waiting!

Free Resources

Hey there, superstar!

You've made it through the book, and I'm so proud of you. But let's be real - reading is just the first step. Now it's time to put all this good stuff into practice. And because I'm not about to send you out there empty-handed, I've got some awesome resources to help you on your journey.

Think of these as your anger management toolkit. They're like the Swiss Army knife of emotional growth - versatile, handy, and they might just save you in a pinch (though maybe don't try to use them to open a can or cut down a small tree).

To access the resources, simply create your free account at www.youarenotcalled.com.

Inside, you'll have to the above resources plus much more!

Inside The Member's Area You'll Find:

- **Scripture Guide for Anger Management** It's packed with verses to help you find peace when you're about to lose your cool.

- **Daily Reflection Journal:** Ready to dig deeper into your anger triggers and responses? Our 30-day Daily Reflection Journal is here to guide you. It's like having a therapist in your pocket, minus the hefty bill.

- **Anger Management Action Plan Template** Time to put those strategies into action! Our Anger Management Action Plan Template will help you create a personalized roadmap to calmer days.

- **"Calm Down" Toolkit** Need a quick cool-down? Our 'Calm Down' Toolkit is your one-stop shop for de-escalating anger in the heat of the moment.

- **Relationship Repair Worksheet** Oops, did your anger cause some relationship hiccups? Our Relationship Repair Worksheet is here to help you smooth things over.

- **Generational Patterns Workbook** Ready to break free from your family's anger legacy? Our Generational Patterns Workbook will guide you through identifying and addressing those inherited anger habits.

- **Physical Relaxation Techniques Cheat Sheet** Want a quick reference guide for all those body-based calming techniques? Our Physical Relaxation Techniques Cheat Sheet has got you covered.

- **Prayer Guide for Overcoming Anger** Need some divine intervention in your anger management journey? Our Prayer Guide for Overcoming Anger is here to help you connect with God and find His peace.

Get access to everything above plus extras for free at www.YouAreNotCalled.com

www.ingramcontent.com/pod-product-compliance
Ingram Content Group UK Ltd.
Pitfield, Milton Keynes, MK11 3LW, UK
UKHW062006290726
14090UKWH00022B/1414

9 781966 130000